NO CONTACT

Ending A Destructive Relationship

Penny L. Haider

Outskirts Press, Inc.
Denver, Colorado

The opinions expressed in this manuscript are solely the opinions of the author and do not represent the opinions or thoughts of the publisher. The author represents and warrants that she either owns or has the legal right to publish all material in this book.

No Contact
Ending A Destructive Relationship
All Rights Reserved.
Copyright © 2008 Penny L. Haider
V9.0R5.1

Cover Photo © 2008 JupiterImages Corporation. All rights reserved - used with permission.

This book may not be reproduced, transmitted, or stored in whole or in part by any means, including graphic, electronic, or mechanical without the express written consent of the publisher except in the case of brief quotations embodied in critical articles and reviews.

Outskirts Press, Inc.
http://www.outskirtspress.com

ISBN: 978-1-4327-1563-2

Library of Congress Control Number: 2007937107

Outskirts Press and the "OP" logo are trademarks belonging to Outskirts Press, Inc.

PRINTED IN THE UNITED STATES OF AMERICA

Table of Contents

Foreword i

Chapter 1 Why the Need for No Contact 1
    The Need for No Contact 1
    The Relationship Is Bad for You 3
    Boundary Violators 4
    Name-Calling 7
    Masters of Confusion 9
    Signs of an Abusive Relationship 12
    You Have a High Probability of Going Back to an
        Abusive Relationship if You Maintain Contact 14
    Breaking It Off 15
    Maintaining Boundaries with No Contact 16
    Gaining Equilibrium with No Contact 17
    Contact Keeps You Vulnerable 18
    Contact Gives You an Excuse to Stay 19

Chapter 2 Getting Out of the Picture 21
    Planning for Your Safety 21
    Get Your Bearings 22
    Stay Calm 23
    Stay in the Moment 24
    Avoid Impulsive Thoughts to Make Contact 24
    Carry a Cell Phone 25

    Keep Yourself and Your Residence Safe 26
    Accept That You May Be Indecisive for Awhile 27
    Keep in Touch with Supportive Friends and Family and
        Use Your Resources! 28
    Remind Yourself You're a Great Person 28

Chapter 3 Keeping Your Cool While Staying Away .. 31
    The Need to Stay Away 31
    Stay Away to Get Used to Not Hearing His Voice.............32
    Stay Away so You Can Evaluate Your Circumstances 33
    Pick Up the Pieces of Your Life 34
    Listen to Yourself 35
    Believe Your Own Thoughts 36
    Take Care of Yourself 37
    Stay Away and Focus on Your Healing..............................38

Chapter 4 Moving Forward…Alone for Awhile 41
    Being Alone 41
    Doing Things You Like to Do 43
    Take Yourself Out 43
    Volunteer Your Time……Even Just a Little..................... 45
    Stay in the Moment and Smile 46
    Take Time to Do Nothing 47
    Have Fun 48
    Discover Your Best Qualities 49
    Your Best Qualities 50
    Observing Yourself 52

Chapter 5 Processing the Loss and Making Changes .. 55
    Back Flashes 55
    I Heard That Song and It Reminded Me of 57
    As Time Passes 58
    Observing Other People 58
    Think about the Role You Played 63
    I Will Never Choose This Again! Avoid Becoming a Target..... 65
    What Are Red Flags? 66
    Reflections 68

Chapter 6 You're Unique! 69
Believe in Yourself 69
You Are the Authority on You 71
You Know What You Are Thinking 72
Your Opinion Matters 74
Who Am I? 76
This Is What I Look Like 77
Your Interests and Passions 78
Checking in on the No Contact 82

Chapter 7 Listening to Yourself 85
Journaling 85
Journaling about Career Changes 86
Be Honest with Yourself When You Write 87
Sometimes Keeping Your Hopes and Dreams to
 Yourself Is a Good Idea 88
Daydreaming Can Be Very Healthy and Enlightening 90
Listening to Yourself as You Talk to Others 91
Do I Always Have to Agree with Others? 94
You Are Changing Your Thought Patterns 96

Chapter 8 But I Still Care about This Person 99
Do You Care about the Person or the Dream? 99
Staying Can Cause You Physical Harm 100
Addicted to the Relationship? 101
Find Outlets for Your Caring Nature 103
Ten Causes I Care About 105
Don't Forget to Care about Yourself First 106

Chapter 9 Relapsing 109
Don't Beat Yourself Up about Making Contact 109
What Prompted the Call? 111
How Did the Call Go? 111
After the Call 112
If You Made Plans to Meet 112
It Was Great for Awhile; Now I'm Back Where I Started 113
Panicking 113

Chapter 10 Getting Back on the Horse 117
Moving Forward Again 117
More Resolve with No Contact 118
Relax 118
Finding Joy 119
Pursue Your Own Adventures 120
Being Different 121

Chapter 11 In a Hurry for Love? 123
Know Who Your Are 123
Addicted to Love 124
The Attraction Factor 126
Learn to Say No 127
Zero Tolerance for Abuse 129
Stating Opinions 130
You've Met Someone New 131
How Do You Feel? 132
Early Red Flags 133
Avoid Becoming Sidetracked 134
Appearances Can Be Deceiving 136
Background Checks 139
Balance in the Relationship 140

Chapter 12 Testing 1, 2, 3 143
Remember to Live Your Life 143
Use Your Head! 144
Physical Intimacy in a New Relationship 145
Communication 145
Rejection 146
When You Reject 148
Life Isn't Always Exciting but It Is a Precious Gift 149

Final Thoughts 153

Traits Associated with Narcissistic Personality Disorder ... 155

Resources for Getting Out of a Destructive Relationship .. 155

Disclaimer

Please seek the advice of a professional before making changes in your current situation. This book is based primarily on personal experiences. The author assumes no responsibility for any outcome of applying the information in this book. If you are in a violent relationship please call a domestic-abuse hotline.

Foreword

Making a life partner choice is the most important decision we ever make. Our health and happiness hinge on that one decision. The wrong choice can cost us financially, for sure, but more importantly, it can suck the life out of us, taking us up and down an emotional roller coaster, and playing havoc with our physical, mental, and spiritual health. The happiest people are the ones who are either single or are in a great relationship with a partner who values them. I used to make partner choices based on attraction and the man showing an interest. Sometimes I avoided approaching a potential partner out of fear of rejection. Too often I would wait for a man to approach me. If I had doubt about a particular partner, I tried hard to ignore it. I didn't fully understand that consistently making good dating choices was critical to my overall personal health and happiness. I lived each day not really grasping the concept of being an independent thinking individual. I stayed busy going to school, working, and eventually raising children, but didn't take enough time to care for and get to know myself. I lived my life according to what others thought was best and was validated by the approval I received from every other person in my life except me. I wasn't able to associate the concept of red flags and boundaries into my personal situation consistently. If I suspected someone was violating one of my boundaries and wanted them in my life, I adjusted to the boundary violation in order to keep that particular person around. Even when I absolutely knew one of my boundaries had been violated, I often looked the other way.

When I was forty-six I left my nineteen year marriage after five years of counseling and a one and a half year divorce process. After the divorce was final ending contact with my ex-husband was difficult because my children wanted their dad to participate in some of our activities. My effort to accommodate them undermined me because I wasn't developing clear boundaries. Within a month the contact with my ex-husband became minimal. I spoke to him over the phone regarding the children and their schedules, social activities, school functions, and parent meetings. The communication has remained this way.

Two years after my divorce I began dating. One person I was in a relationship with was an active alcoholic. It took me six months to fully see the alcoholism and once I did see it, I plunged into Al-Anon. I was bound and determined to be the best girlfriend I could be to this man. It took me a long time to completely let go. Once I did, I examined my direction and the relationship choices I was making and realized I was in serious jeopardy of losing the ability to care for myself and my children as well as maintain viable employment. I forced myself to end the relationship. I ended communication by changing my cell phone number, unplugging my landline for several weeks, eventually changing my home phone number, and moving.

At the age of fifty-one I picked myself up and little by little changed the way I lived my life. I made more time to read about self-discovery, self-examination, and relationships. I also took more time to be still and less time keeping busy. I believed that my being as busy as I had been played a major part in my inability to understand myself, my boundaries, and in turn, relate better to others. Once I took the time to think about what I needed and wanted I was able to retrain myself to take care of my needs. I realized that living a good life isn't difficult but it does take self-discipline. I also learned I'm as important as other people and deserve to be treated as well as I would treat anyone else. What followed has been a blessing. I learned that my company is good company. I also learned I can say no to another person and feel okay with it. I can set a boundary and keep it. If they don't like it and go away, I will survive and be just fine.

Sometimes we gravitate toward those who treat us the worst because we don't believe we deserve better. If this is the case for you, the only way to realize you deserve to be treated well is to retrain yourself to expect respect. It requires knowing what you will and won't accept from other people and firmly setting those boundaries. I used to think there was something defective about me because I didn't get the respect I felt I deserved. I didn't realize I was training people to treat me poorly. I had weak boundaries and would often feel guilty if I did stand up and tell people what I wanted. I thought that being a person with boundaries was too rigid. I didn't understand that knowing what I would and wouldn't accept gave me the boundaries I needed to live life successfully. I believed that standing up for myself and expecting better behavior was a sure way to push everyone away. I felt it was best to be nice and keep smiling no matter what. Consequently, I put the needs and wants of others ahead of my own.

This book is intended to be used as a source by those who are leaving or plan to leave a destructive relationship. I am not a licensed psychologist, psychiatrist, or social worker. I am a woman who has experienced years of partner abuse and wants to help others.

If you are considering leaving your current partner, it is necessary for your safety and well being to have a plan of action, and to check it out with those you trust and/or a licensed mental health specialist. If the possibility exists that you are putting yourself in danger, direction from law enforcement officials may also be necessary.

None of us need to be in a partnership with another person. It isn't absolutely necessary though it is wonderful to have someone to share life with. A destructive relationship leaves you feeling drained and with the belief your needs aren't important. You end up viewing relationships as a lot of hard work with little joy. You spend your time adapting to the needs of others and placing yourself in uncomfortable and/or risky situations on a regular basis. You might be taking part in a lot of game playing to prove your love. This could include: chasing, running away, calculating, manipulating, or dramatizing. You may feel isolated, suffer from loneliness, feel shame, or are scared. Maybe you are dealing with ongoing physical abuse. You may feel confused and bewildered while attempting to rationalize things that have been said or done. You might also have an ongoing sinking or stabbing feeling in your gut that doesn't go away. There is a way of breaking free from a destructive relationship and the self-destructive behavior patterns which allow these types of relationships to flourish.

By making *you* a priority, and accepting yourself fully, you can create a better life. You will live better by getting to know and accepting who you are before attempting to create a partnership with another person.

It is my sincere hope that by sharing my views, suggestions for healing, and some of my personal experiences, you will be encouraged toward removing yourself from a destructive relationship.

Chapter 1
Why the Need for No Contact?

The Need for No Contact

No doubt about it, some people in this world are lethal. They have no regard whatsoever for others. Their objective is to get what they want when they want it from whom they want it.

For those of us who have been in abusive relationships the recovery process is hard. It takes so much time to put the pieces of us back together because these pieces were slowly and deliberately taken from us over time. In order to heal, we've got to pick these pieces up and reconnect them to make ourselves whole.

In the early days of my healing I read at length about abuse. I learned that although there are different types of abusers they all lack empathy for others. I also found in my reading that personality disorders were often mentioned alongside discussions about abusers. When I came across Narcissistic Personality Disorder and the traits associated with it, I was amazed by how familiar it all sounded. Narcissists are usually drawn to people they believe are unique or have special qualities. This is important to them because they believe they are special and should only associate with people worthy of them. They also want to impress the outside world so want to make sure whoever they associate with helps them look good to others. They might be drawn to people with intelligence, money, fame, position, power, beauty or combinations of these and other qualities they deem desirable. They and other abusive individuals tend to pick partners who lack confidence, have low self-esteem, and have wavering boundaries or no boundaries at all. In the beginning their charm and wit are hard to resist and they pursue a new partner with a vengeance. However, over time they lose interest in the relationship. They often become distant and uncommunicative as well as mentally emotionally and/or physically abusive.

I was first introduced to the concept of no contact through my readings at an online discussion group: NarcissisticPersonalityGroup@groups.msn.com. At this group I learned that in order to leave an abusive relationship you must eliminate all contact. However keeping the no contact rule is different when sharing co-parenting responsibilities or in an employment setting. In these cases the contact must be kept to a minimum as it relates to the children or to the workplace.

It isn't easy to leave a destructive relationship; especially if you aren't used to standing up for yourself. Your biggest ally in doing this will be your resolve to have the best life possible. Whenever you weaken, remember your happiness depends on taking care of yourself first. Also keep your thinking reality based. You are more vulnerable if you have a fantasy view toward life. It's to an abuser's advantage to find a partner who longs for a prince to sweep them off their feet. This is how they reel you in. Women planted firmly in reality aren't looking for a prince and won't buy into the fantasy. This doesn't mean that a woman should run from a man who treats her well but should be wary of a man who appears too good too soon. Chances are they're giving a great performance which won't be repeated once he's convinced he's won her over.

The Relationship Is Bad for You

Simply put, you've decided you don't want contact with this person because it is bad for you! Your self-esteem is on the line and to heal you've got to stay away. It may take awhile to decide you want to end the relationship. It's a difficult decision with much to consider. When in a relationship with a narcissist, they want you to do what they want, when they want it. If it turns out you actually want to do what they want on a regular basis, it becomes too much like sharing, and they won't want it anymore. In other words, you won't reach a level of mutual sharing and understanding. You might wonder why things don't seem quite right. Maybe you get a sick feeling in the pit of your stomach then shrug it off, rationalizing you're too sensitive or didn't understand what was said or done. Men and women in these relationships often report that although they share some great times with their partner, they spend far more time feeling uneasy or downright miserable. Maybe you've hesitated bringing up your feelings, fearing that doing so, will anger your partner. Feeling hesitant and fearful of sharing emotion shouldn't be part of a healthy relationship.

Boundary Violators

Narcissists have no interest in boundaries, period. As was mentioned above, they are attracted to people who don't have firm boundaries. The abuser may be physically, mentally, and/or emotionally abusive. Their objective is to get their way, no matter what. In the beginning of these relationships life can look and seems good. These individuals can be quite charming and accommodating initially. Over time though, they may view the relationship as less exciting and you will never get them back to the full form they first presented. Chances are if you continue to stay in the relationship you'll get used to accepting poor behavior over and over again. If you accept poor behavior even one time and don't put an end to it you're leaving yourself wide open for more abuse. In my past, I wasn't consistently clear about my boundaries and consequently didn't always stand up for myself. Sometimes I wasn't even aware I was being violated until it was too late:

On my birthday, shortly after my divorce was final, three of my children who were spending the weekend with their dad, came over with him to bring me a bouquet of flowers and a birthday cake. I put the flowers in a vase and set them on the kitchen table. We all gathered around the table and I stretched toward the flowers to smell them and then looked up. My ex-husband told me to smell the flowers again. I said no; he said "come on smell them again," and pushed my head into the bouquet with his hand. When I lifted my head he looked at me and laughed out loud. I went into the bathroom, looked in the mirror, and saw residue from the flowers all over my face. I was being made a joke of on my birthday, in front of my children! I came out of the bathroom and told my ex-husband to leave.

In hindsight, I should have paid attention to my first thought and walked away. Instead, I allowed him to push my head into the bouquet. I didn't understand

and process in the moment that having my head pushed into the flowers was a violation. Hesitating and ignoring my own feelings made me vulnerable. When a person lacks confidence they can be directed to do things a person with clear boundaries wouldn't consider doing. Learn to stand up for yourself whether you're at home, at a family gathering, or in a business meeting.

Sometimes in a new relationship we make a decision to accept the unacceptable. We accommodate a new person in order to keep them in our lives. We don't want to pass judgment so ignore our boundaries. We forget to pay attention to our wants and needs concentrating only on pleasing the other person. Here is an example from my personal experience:

Three years after my divorce I began a new relationship with a man who told me from the beginning he didn't like being questioned and wasn't very "revealing" about daily happenings in his life. I took his upfront disclosure policy seriously and decided I would do my best to ignore anything I suspected to be a lie or half truth. Above all, I made it a point not to ask questions or limit the questions I did ask! I had been taught not to pry into other people's business and accept what they told me. I was the perfect partner for this no disclosure policy boyfriend! This mindset had undermined me throughout adulthood but proved especially detrimental in this particular rela-

tionship. I made up my mind to rarely question anything he told me. It took a long time to see that by accepting the bits and pieces of his life he chose to give me and by not asking questions I really didn't have a relationship. I didn't know him and I was losing sight of myself. Eventually I realized a healthy relationship doesn't look like this. It took nearly losing all interest in my own life to take the necessary steps to get out. I had stopped valuing and believing in myself. My universe centered on this mans wants and needs. If he was okay then I was okay. He was the barometer for how things were going in my own life.

Pay attention to your own wants and needs. If you have the gut feeling things aren't right in your relationship, it's a good indicator you need to get to the bottom of whatever is making you feel uneasy. If you let things slide even once, it will become easier to continue to let things go rather than confronting the issues head on. It's impossible to have a good relationship without communication. If you're in a relationship where your questions are met with silence, are ignored, or you're redirected to another topic of conversation, don't ignore these behaviors.

Name-Calling

If you have come out of a destructive relationship, chances are, you have gotten used to being put down verbally. Name-calling is the use of any negative label to describe another person. Abusers probably think they have the right to put their partner down for a variety of reasons: they may be older, are the breadwinner, have more education, or feel they are superior in some other way. Narcissists have a strong sense of entitlement which blinds them to their abusive behavior. Most abusers also believe they can say things to other people that they themselves would never be able to tolerate. They lack the ability to acknowledge and accept their partner's feelings, perspectives, and opinions if they are different from their own. Verbal abuse creates pain and trauma. It can make you physically ill. Ongoing verbal abuse is stressful no matter how much you try to ignore it. On the other hand, non abusers will occasionally say something cruel because they are upset or frustrated, and when they think about how they came across, will apologize. The rare hurtful comment made when frustrated is different from the ongoing remarks made by an abusive individual.

In the early days of one relationship, I was often told I was wonderful, exciting, fun, etc. However, over time, the positive regards were expressed less and less. One evening we were on our way to dinner when he slipped something into my jacket pocket. I reached in my pocket and pulled out a magazine clipping. It was a poem about a woman who though not at all exciting was a comfort to be around. He told me the poem reminded him of me.

No Contact

At the time, I brushed the whole thing aside, even though reading the poem and hearing his reasoning for giving it to me gave me a sick feeling in the pit of my stomach. I should have paid attention to the way I felt. The sick feeling was my body's way of telling me that neither the poem nor comment was okay with me. Yet in the moment, I pretended everything was fine. I didn't want him to think I was bothered at all after reading it. By saying nothing I allowed him to get away with treating me poorly. I disregarded the pain I was feeling by denying it. After the relationship ended the poem became significant as clear use of devaluation.

How much self have you allowed another person to take from you? Do you know when enough is enough?

Remember, anyone who calls you names or in some other way attempts to devalue and make you feel inferior has no regard for you. It's about keeping you down. Don't get used to these comments. Remember to expect respect! Stay sharp and don't allow others to put you down because over time, it will wear you out.

Masters of Confusion

Narcissists tend to change on a daily basis. If there is one consistency in their personalities it's that they are unpredictable and extremely changeable. What worked for them yesterday will most likely not work the next day. They often expect a partner to be able to read their moods and know instinctively what it is they need at any moment. Your wants and needs don't factor into the equation unless giving you what you need and want helps them portray a desirable image to the outside world. Their catch phrase might be "you make me feel…." The problem is you could make them feel alive and wonderful one day and like they're hooked to a ball and chain the next. You will most likely not be able to predict what each new day will bring. There were times in my past relationships when I considered myself to be in ongoing train wrecks. I knew a wreck was coming, however didn't know from which direction, or the force of impact upon crashing.

The confusion we feel with abusers is a deliberate control mechanism. If you listen to what they say and try to make sense out of it, you get caught up in the confusion. The trick is not to allow them to confuse you. The easiest way to do this is by not responding. Get out, stay away, don't contact.

With one ex-boyfriend, I could be in a great mood, thoroughly excited and anticipating our time together. One time in particular we were in the car. I was quiet, just enjoying the drive. He said, "Are you

okay, is everything alright?" I assured him I was fine and then he added:
"I'm bored."
"Why?" I asked. "We have nothing to talk about anymore," he said.

This exchange was used to let me know it was my responsibility to keep the conversation going so he felt comfortable. It wasn't okay for me to be still, to be quiet, unless he wanted me to. I worried about whether my behavior was acceptable at any given moment in relationship to his moods. During this particular car ride I was anxious and unsure of his reaction to my continued silence so picked up on his cue to start talking. By doing this, I let him off the hook. I did what I was supposed to do which was to create conversation in order for him to feel less uncomfortable. I got nothing out of this exchange except an awareness that he was in control. I played the part I was supposed to play.

It isn't anyone's responsibility to keep another person entertained. We're capable of doing that for ourselves. However, some very charming and persuasive people are used to calling the shots and getting results. People with a strong sense of entitlement think nothing of expecting partners and others to follow their lead, agree with their views, and succumb to their wishes.

Signs of an Abusive Relationship

There will be other sections which show warning signs and red flags to be aware of when looking at a new relationship partner. Here you look at your current relationship and note whether or not any or all of the following apply:

- Is possessive or jealous toward you.
- Bossy or demanding in attempts to control you.
- May have a quick temper and/or is violent.
- Attempts to isolate you by cutting you off from friends, family, and other social contacts.
- Abuses alcohol and/or drugs.
- You feel pressure sexually and/or demands sexual activities you're not comfortable with.
- Tells you you're responsible when he mistreats you.
- History of bad relationships.
- Friends and family are concerned for your health and safety.
- You worry about your partner's reactions to what you say and do.
- Partner makes "jokes" that embarrass, humiliate, or shame you privately or around family and friends.
- Partner has angry outbursts when they feel hurt, shame, fear, or loss of control.
- Partner witnessed abusive parental relationship and/or was abused as a child.
- In order to cope with the pain of the relationship, you and/or your partner have developed or pro-

gressed in alcohol or drug dependence.
- You repeatedly leave and return to relationship against the advice of your loved ones.
- You are not able to leave the relationship even though you know it is in your best interests to do so.

If you are thinking about leaving a destructive disturbing or otherwise unworkable relationship know you'll most likely always struggle with claiming a sense of self while with this person. It will zap you of your energy and for all your effort you'll still feel a sense of loss and emptiness. If your partner agrees to couples therapy and both of you are sincerely interested in making positive changes then go for it. Just be prepared that it might not work and in the end you'll need to get out so you can begin living a normal life.

Remember to expect respect. It takes practice, and trust in yourself, to know when something someone says to you, or wants you to do, isn't right. Stand up for yourself and realize you have great value. Don't let other people push you around, embarrass, or in some other way make you feel inferior. People who are cruel to you are not worth having in your life. Above all, don't be so dependent on another person, that the value you place on yourself is determined by the attention they pay to you. You are a separate person!

You Have a High Probability of Going Back to an Abusive Relationship if You Maintain Contact

Yes you do but if you're still in the relationship there's no need to panic. Timing plays a critical role when you begin the process of leaving. You may have been in a relationship with this person for years and if so you'll need to detach. Detaching is important when you can't completely shut a person out of your life. If you have children with an abusive individual there will usually be some contact. There are also destructive relationships with people other than intimate partners. You might have a difficult relationship with a coworker, and in that case, it's often impossible to avoid contact altogether unless you quit your job. Whether you're in a co-parenting situation, or the relationship is with a co-worker, maintain only minimal necessary contact.

If you've decided to leave a destructive relationship it may initially seem normal to continue contact with your former partner. However, it seems normal only because it is familiar. If you choose to stay in the relationship you can continue to work on yourself, though it may be difficult because your partner is still in the picture. It will be a delicate balance to give time and energy to you while continuing on in the relationship. Your concentration will be divided and it will be difficult to divert the time and energy you formally gave to your partner onto yourself.

In addition, it's likely you'll slip into previously set patterns you had with your partner and if you attempt to break these patterns will be met with resistance. Positive changes can happen but both you and your partner must be committed to the change. You are also likely to need guidance from a mental health specialist. It would be easier for you to clear your mind and space of this person before working on changing your own behavior patterns.

Breaking It Off

Breaking away from a destructive relationship is tough because even though it was dysfunctional it held value and a certain amount of enjoyment for you or you wouldn't have been in it at all. The objective of leaving is to bring peace and joy back into your life as well as to gain control of your world.

Destructive relationships are not joyful. There may be brief periods of happiness but overall there is a greater amount of dissatisfaction and misery. To settle for that type of relationship is crazy which is why you want out.

If you choose to move forward with no contact you

will need to make adjustments. It will be nearly impossible to stay away in the beginning but over time it will become easier as long as you maintain self-discipline.

Maintaining Boundaries with No Contact

Without clear boundaries none of us have a solid foundation to build on. We all know and understand this however putting it into practice is hard work.

Knowing who you are, accepting it, and growing with it, are the keys to developing a life you truly enjoy. If you are convinced that leaving the partnership is the best course of action to take, you will need to set your boundaries. This will be difficult. He may call you. He may come to see you. What do you do? You know the person and your situation. If you believe it's safe to do so, you could say the following: Please find someone else on whom to focus your attention as I have no interest in you at all. Saying this allows the other person to keep their dignity because if that is stripped away, it could mean misery and danger for you. To say anymore than the above just sucks you back in.

Once you have made it clear you're no longer interested don't take their calls and don't open the door to them. If the phone rings let the answering machine pick it up. If the calls continue save the messages as you may need them for evidence. You may also want to consider getting another phone with an unlisted number and use that phone only with close friends and family.

When I left the last relationship I was committed to no contact but felt vulnerable and knew I would be tempted to pick up the phone if he called. I decided to unplug my landline using it only when necessary. I kept in touch with friends and family by using a cell phone with a number only they knew. I went to work every day and took care of my children. It was more important for me to self-protect than to worry about whether or not I was available to answer my phone.

Gaining Equilibrium with No Contact

Equilibrium is a state of balance. When we're in a state of balance we feel good about ourselves and the way we live our lives. If you are in an abusive relationship much of your energy is used to keep the relationship going. You are out of balance because too much of your energy is being poured into another person who isn't bringing positive energy back to you. It's possible to maintain the relationship and shift energy to you but it will take self-discipline and discernment to do so. The other issue is your partner's reaction to your newly found interest in taking care of yourself. How will they deal with it? How will you deal with their reaction? Both partners in a relationship deserve to have a stable life with another person. It may be possible to improve the relationship for a short time but without ongoing counseling and commitment to change by both people, your energy will most likely be used to maintain status quo.

Contact Keeps You Vulnerable

Let's say that Sally left a relationship on Friday; three days later her ex-partner calls. Sally is sad and misses him so decides to pick up the phone when he calls. She had made it through three days without contact. After the call she set herself back three days. She's depressed and has him on her mind again. It really doesn't matter what was said during the conversation; she lost ground. She goes three more days and recovers from the first phone call, just begins to stabilize, and gets another call. She is now back where she was six days before when she got the first call.

When you pick up the phone, you're still involved and thinking about your ex-partner. You lose focus on what you're trying to accomplish which is to move forward. Instead the focus is switched back to them.

No Contact

Contact Gives You an Excuse to Stay

It is familiar to stay inside the relationship. Life will not feel normal once you leave. You need to adapt to this change and remember that change never feels normal in the beginning.

In the early days after my divorce, my life didn't feel normal at all. I went through the motions. At the time, I worked as a substitute teacher. One day I remember standing in a classroom thinking, this isn't me, where did I go? I still did the same things every day but it felt like I was living someone else's life. It felt surreal. It took a long time before I was able to accept that, yes, this is my life.

It is also difficult to leave the other people behind who were part of your life as a result of the relationship you were in. These other people may include your partner's children, friends, relatives, and co-workers. You may also be leaving special pets behind. Sometimes it may be more difficult to lose contact with the other individuals than with the actual relationship partner. However, at this time, the most important people in your life are you and your own children, if you have children. Your ex-partner may even enlist the help of these other people to drag you back into the relationship. Be aware of this, and act accordingly. It is again in your best interest to limit or cut off contact with others who are directly involved with your ex-partner. You may believe it is cruel to do this but when you stop and think about it, what will you gain by keeping in touch with them? Are you doing it because you genuinely want them in your life? Are you in touch with them in hopes you will learn more about what is happening with your ex? Who he is seeing, what he is doing? How will having this information benefit you in terms of your own healing? How will having this information help you move on? If you are committed to no contact, you need to break away from your ex-partner and the other people who are significant to them. If the relationship you're leaving is with an ex-spouse or partner and you have children together, it's not likely you'll cut off all contact. The objective will be to have limited contact with your ex. Contact with your ex-partner will be necessary regarding your children's health, safety, and scheduling concerns. It's unnecessary to continue regular contact with your ex, their friends, and other family members for any other reason.

Chapter 2

Getting Out of the Picture

Planning for Your Safety

Whether you've been in a long or short term relationship with the person you are choosing to leave, safety planning is essential; however, if you are in immediate danger you should dial 911. If you can't get to a phone as the abuse is happening, get out as soon as you can.

You will need advice and support from others which include community resources and maybe local law enforcement. They can instruct you on how to be safe while disconnecting from the relationship. Be sure the plan you use is realistic. If you need help getting back on your feet there are safe houses and shelters where you can live. Court advocates can help you file charges and take out restraining orders if needed. They can also help you with child support enforcement or food stamps as well as counseling services. Support groups are available to help you with the healing process; legal aid services can help with legal issues; city and county housing services are also available. There is no need to suffer through your transition in silence when there are many resources available to help you.

Even though you will have resources a good portion of your time will involve you, on your own, as you move you and your family toward better lives. The remaining information in this chapter offers suggestions of things you can do to keep you and your family safe.

Get Your Bearings

If you decide you want to leave a destructive relationship determine what you need to do to keep yourself and if you have children, keep all of you safe and with a place to call home. This first step is often the hardest. You may initially need to find a temporary home. Keep telling yourself it's only temporary in order to continue moving forward. It can be frustrating to be in a short term living situation whether it is in a shelter or staying with friends and family. Just stay focused on your goal of independence. Once you feel stable you can establish your new life one step at a time. Be patient and give yourself time to determine your long range goals. Chances are if you were in a relationship with an abusive individual, you weren't 100 percent clear about what you want in life.

If you are committed to leaving a person you no longer want contact with its most likely because you realized at some point that this person is toxic to you. They don't look at life the same way you do. They don't want what you want, refuse to see your point of view, and have no desire to compromise. They may be physically, emotionally, mentally, or sexually abusive. Coming out of this type of relationship can leave you feeling like you don't know which way is up.

Stay Calm

In order to leave a relationship you've been compulsive about channel your energy to stay calm, away from this person, and on your own. Filling the void will initially feel like a huge challenge to overcome. Even if you are working and/or raising children the emptiness will sometimes seem overwhelming. Instead of rushing to fill up the void accept it. Accepting your circumstances will keep you calm and calming down is important because you need to establish roots inside your own life.

When I left my last relationship I read a lot. I also walked regularly and found the walking and other exercise helped keep me focused on my recovery. In addition, I spent time with my sons watching DVD's, going to basketball games, and just hanging out.

Stay in the Moment

Staying in the moment keeps your thoughts focused in the here and now. Be careful not to get swept up in feelings of longing and reminiscing. If you do daydream about your ex-partner allow yourself a set amount of time; say five minutes. Then be ready to switch gears and think about the present. Prepare dinner or begin that great book you've wanted to read. Go on the bike ride you and your child have talked about. Stay focused on the activity you are in at the moment. Take stock in your positive steps. What you're doing in the moment matters because it's part of what is going on in your life right now!

Avoid Impulsive Thoughts to Make Contact

Even though you have committed to staying away from this person there will be times when you want to break your commitment. You may get the urge to make contact because you felt a twinge of sorrow or loneliness or lost interest in an activity. Maybe you have a flashback of a pleasant memory; or something you or someone else did or said, reminds you of your ex-partner. Think about whatever idea comes to mind for a couple of minutes then let it go. Continue with what you're doing in the present.

When you feel the impulse to make contact:
Go for a walk
Read the paper, a magazine, a book
Play with your kids
Soak in the tub
Turn on the TV
Turn on the radio
Dance
Work on a jigsaw or crossword puzzle
Call a friend – however avoid talking about your ex
Brush your teeth
Sing a silly song
Play with your pet

The objective is to stay in the moment. Concentrate on getting through the next five minutes then the next five after that. Be gentle with yourself but consistently move forward with your healing.

Carry a Cell Phone

If you can't afford a cell phone contact a community women's agency. Some agencies will supply them for free. You shouldn't have to pay for a cell phone plan if you have the phone for emergencies only. You should also be able to call 911 from any cell phone at no cost. Make sure your phone is charged so it always has power and keep it within reach at all times.

Keep Yourself and Your Residence Safe

For many months there were various signs of trespassing outside my home. There were also more than a few nights when my children and I were awakened by the sounds of banging on the exterior of the house and then a car driving away. I kept a log of these occurrences and also made contact with the local police. Eventually, I installed a security system. After installing the system the problems I was having were eliminated.

You may want to consider the following safety measures in order to keep yourself safe if your ex-partner is exhibiting threatening behaviors.

- Consider moving—it may save your life.
- Inform family, friends, neighbors, co-workers, yours and/or your children's schools, and describe the threatening person and the vehicle they drive.
- Avoid going out alone especially at night and park in well-lit areas.
- Always carry a cell phone.
- Install deadbolt locks on your outside doors and make sure the doors can't be kicked in.

No Contact

- Install motion detector lights outside your home especially in dark areas.
- Trim shrubs near doors and consider planting thorny shrubs under windows.
- Keep your windows doors garage and fence gates locked.
- Install curtains or blinds that make it impossible to see inside your house.
- Install a peephole in your door to identify visitors.
- Invest in a security system. There are excellent plans out there that are reasonably priced.

Accept That You May Be Indecisive for Awhile

Being indecisive comes with making a life change. Things are different; there is less clarity in everything you do. Don't fight it; accept it. It will pass. You are changing a pattern of accepting unacceptable behavior and learning to choose a healthier way of living. In the beginning it can be difficult to create this type of change because it is hard to know what healthier people look like.

When I first came out of my last relationship, I walked around in a daze. I felt fragile and was thankful I worked with many people who were pleasant and kind. I didn't make huge decisions during this time but instead read a lot and reflected daily. I got used to my life in the here and now--going to work, taking care of my-

self and family, helping with homework, and attending school functions. These were really the only things I was able to handle at the time.

Keep in Touch with Supportive Friends and Family and Use Your Resources!

We all need to feel we are connected and during this time it's especially important to know there are people we can turn to. Be selective but stay connected. Do your best not to talk at length about your ex-partner. Lengthy conversations about him create the illusion he is still in your life. You want others to know you are creating a new life and you'll feel better the less time spent talking about your ex with friends and family. You do want to process the memories from the relationship but at this time you're better off not talking at length about your ex. There are other things to talk about: your children, work, the weather, current events, just keep your thoughts focused on the present. If you have a limited number of friends and family available please remember to use your community resources. Keep them handy and use them often. There are resources at the end of this book which can be of help.

Remind Yourself You're a Great Person!

You are! Not only do you need the support of

No Contact

friends and family during this time, you need support from yourself.

Believe in yourself! Stick post-its up to remind yourself that you're doing a great job while at work. Smile at others. Smiling makes you feel better.

Treat yourself to something special. Get a massage, manicure, or pedicure. Have lunch with a friend; go out to a movie. Remember that in order to take care of yourself, you have got to be a TOP priority!

You're making a commitment to you at this time and must follow through. The next chapter deals with the subject of keeping your cool while staying away. So take some time right now to relax.

Chapter 3

Keeping Your Cool While Staying Away

The Need to Stay Away

Again, if you choose to stay rather than leave a destructive relationship, you will most likely slip back into old patterns of behavior. If you do decide you must stay in your current situation, do your best to come up with a plan that works for you. As stated in the previous chapter, there are resources. Make sure you use them and plan for your safety. There may be a time in the future when you do decide to leave. If you have planned ahead, leaving will go much smoother.

After leaving, there will most likely be times when you become sentimental and sometimes the anxiety and sadness of having left the relationship take over. Don't allow your emotions to control you. Remember that emotions are just that. Guard against being swept away by your emotions after hearing a song, having a tender memory, or being in a particular location you had been with your partner. Feel the emotion but don't let it control you; do your best to let it go once you feel it. Refer back to the suggestions regarding what you can do when you have the impulse to make contact.

Stay Away to Get Used to Not Hearing His Voice

You don't want to hear this person's voice because it still seems normal to hear it. If you stay away, the familiarity will eventually fade.

Another reason you don't want to hear their voice is because it breaks the concentration you need to give to yourself. If you continue to concentrate on your ex-partner you lose your focus. Often when in a relationship with a narcissist or another abusive type there is only room to accommodate the needs of one person and that person isn't you. The abuser expects you to bend and sway to meet their needs. Your needs and wants aren't usually taken into consideration unless meeting your needs benefits them in some way.

Stay Away so You Can Evaluate Your Circumstances

Developing a better understanding of who you are is of great value to you right now. You want to learn about the role you played in the relationship and what you can do to prevent this type of relationship from ever developing again.

Through conversation with others, workshops, online discussion groups, reading books and articles, journaling, and daily reflection you'll gain knowledge. There is a wealth of information regarding personality disorders and dysfunctional relationships. There is an increasing amount of information about dealing with narcissism. Sam Vaknin is an excellent resource with his book: <u>Malignant Self-Love</u>. There are also online support groups. Learn as much as you can in order to gain insight and discover why you were attracted to this type of individual in the first place.

When I left my last relationship, I was like a sponge soaking up as much information as I could get about narcissism and other personality disorders as well as reading postings from readers at the Narcissistic Personality Disorder online support group. The research I did through reading and making connections with others proved to be invaluable resources and a major factor in my ability to leave the destructive relationship I had been in.

It is absolutely necessary to take enough time to get to know yourself well. I mentioned in the foreword that I got used to staying busy. It seemed that I rushed around getting things done but most of that involved completing tasks. I paid bills, shopped, ran errands, took the kids to their activities etc. I filled my life up with things that kept me busy but didn't take enough time to be still and evaluate what I needed and wanted in life. I was fulfilled by pleasing and doing things for others rather than understanding what would please me. During your transition period take time to think about what you want. Thinking about what you want will actually help you notice new opportunities rather than the lack of opportunity.

Pick Up the Pieces of Your Life

For me, putting my life back in order was a slow process. I got used to living in a fog and not consistently paying attention to what I needed to do for myself and my children. I allowed others to come into my life and take over. I had weak boundaries. I thought I was strong in mind and character, but when I had a partner I didn't stand firm in my boundaries. I felt incomplete by myself so didn't consistently discern an appropriate from an inappropriate person.

I found it easy to accept another person's beliefs

and values as my own. I was quick to denounce my thoughts and see my partner's way as the "right" way. I didn't give myself credit for having good judgment and keen insight. After leaving the last relationship, the fog started to lift. I began to see myself in a new light. I was maintaining no contact and feeling good about myself.

Believe you have the intellectual capacity to make solid decisions. I'm not saying don't pay attention to the opinions of others; do listen. Just don't be too quick to discount your opinion for that of another person. Make decisions, big and small. Making small decisions will encourage you, provide momentum, and give you confidence to make bigger ones.

Listen to Yourself

There will be a chapter devoted to the topic of listening to you. It probably seems obvious that a person should pay attention to his or her own thoughts but sometimes we dismiss what we think as not being clear or accurate.

It's easier to pay attention to our own thoughts when we are by ourselves. We have a captive audience at that point since there is no outside interference. Paying attention to our own thoughts becomes more difficult when we're around others. Sometimes there is a tendency to push aside our opinions in favor of someone else's. We think they may see things more clearly than we do. Although a different perspective can be helpful develop trust in your instincts. Give yourself credit for knowing more about you than anyone else does. Listen to what others have to say but make your own decisions.

Believe Your Own Thoughts

When you don't have this person in your life you will start paying better attention to your own thoughts and views. You will not have another person telling you that you don't know what you're talking about or that you don't know what is best in a particular situation.

In my marriage I often heard that I didn't know anything about work and wouldn't be able to hold down a job because I didn't know what it was like in the real world. I was frequently told that I was too sheltered and too used to being a stay-at-home mom to make in the work world.

Hearing this contributed to my feeling inferior to people who were employed. I was convinced of two things: that I wouldn't find a job, and if I did find one, wouldn't be able to keep it. Consequently I didn't work outside the home for many years. Time slipped by because I had no confidence in my abilities. I had a mental block and really believed I wasn't employable and knew nothing about the world of work.

My voice, the one that thought I was smart and capable became buried farther and farther inside me. I was losing the ability to retrieve this voice and instead paid attention to another person's view of who they thought I was.

Remember:
You can believe you own thoughts.
Believe in the value of your own life experiences.
Trust your instincts.
You do know what you're talking about.
You are smart and capable.
You have value.
Always believe in you!

Take Care of Yourself

It is always our job to take care of ourselves, however, be even more mindful of this now. Create a loving atmosphere for you. Think about what it would take to make a more peaceful setting in your home. It may be as simple as lighting a few candles. If you like certain types of music play it. If there are certain dishes you enjoy cooking make them now. If you would like more pillows for a couch or chair buy them. Anything you do is an added expense so stay within your budget but do something to lighten your mood and create a peaceful living environment. You are worth the attention, will gain new confidence, and be less attracted to individuals who do not offer the same care and kindness to themselves and others.

See the value that you have. No one else will value us if we don't value ourselves.

Stay Away and Focus on Your Healing

I can't think of a more empowering thing to do than to focus on your own healing. Give yourself permission to take care of yourself. If you have children living with you and they are young do what you can to make life easy on yourself for a little while. Prepare easy meals or go out to dinner. Maybe have a friend or relative come over and watch the kids for an evening. Make use of after school programs. Do what is necessary to aid in your healing. If you are working and have health leave available this would be a good time to take some days off. If your children are older, advise them that you need to take care of yourself, and want them to do the meal preparation for a couple of days. Most of the time kids are willing to do this if they've had practice navigating around a kitchen. It also helps if there are supplies, so make sure you have the necessary ingredients and then let them go for it. They will do a good job and you will get time to take care of you.

If you require more sleep then discipline yourself to get to bed earlier. If you have reading to do, take advantage of this time to do it. If you have projects you want to tackle, work on them. Do what you want to do for you. Be gentle with you following the break-up. We often get stuck in the healing process because we take so little time to heal ourselves. Much of our day is taken up being productive on the job, going to school, and taking care of our families. There are also day to day chores, bills to pay, houses to keep in order, and repairs that need to be made. Sure, those things need to get done; but reprioritize to make sure you are at the top of the list. Sometimes we leave a relationship when we're in the middle of a job change. Here is an example from my experience:

I committed to leaving a relationship the day before I was to start a new job. I went to that job in a daze. I didn't think I had enough energy to make it through the day let alone attempt to absorb the mountain of new information and training in front of me. I confided to a fellow employee about my personal situation. She told me something I will never forget. She said: "You have a lot going for you; you don't need that relationship, period. You better focus on this work because it is difficult to learn. Now, stop thinking about what you left, and focus on what's here in front of you!"

Suddenly I bolted to attention. It was surprising to have someone I didn't know well be so candid with me. It made me think twice about what mattered and at that point my life took a turn for the better.

Chapter 4
Moving Forward...Alone for Awhile

Being Alone

Being alone at this time is hard because you're anxious. When you're alone after being in a relationship, even a destructive one, it feels like everyone else is part of a couple. Wherever you go it will seem like the rest of the world is in twos. It only seems that way because you have a sense of urgency to be part of a twosome. Accept that you are alone. It can turn out to be an enlightening time because it will allow you to get to know the most important person in your life, you!

We are not a society that craves time alone. Unless we are alone in a room with no sound, we are likely to be bombarded with noise. It comes from our own voices and those of others. The television radio and traffic are just a few of the sounds we hear day in and day out. It isn't that we should live without sound; however, we do need to nourish ourselves. Diane Kennedy Pike sums it up like this in her article <u>Taking Your Time Alone:</u>

It is a time to remember who you are. It is a time to nourish self as an emerging spirit coming into personal expression. It is a time to assess the state of your character. It is a time of renewal.

We need to pay attention to what is going on inside us and respond to it. When we are alone we can take time to acknowledge the feelings and thoughts occupying our mind. We can guide these thoughts and decide whether to continue to live our lives as we have previously, or redirect out energy in ways which will be more helpful to us.

Purposefully spend time by yourself. Our days are filled with noise. Noise creates stress that keeps our bodies in a state of constant alert. It is difficult to escape sound; however, you can make a point of taking time out and getting away from it as best you can. Your mind needs the stillness and a break from television, radio, voices etc. If you are living in an environment in which there is no way to escape noise, you may want to try a nature sounds cd. There are many varieties to choose from and it may help relax and center you.

Doing Things You Like to Do

It is often easier to get excited about activities when we share them but it's good to have our own interests separate from what we do with others. In a destructive relationship it's not difficult to become so enmeshed in the relationship that we fail to see who we are away from the other person. We think in terms of what our partner wants and needs. It's almost not worth the effort to allow time to explore our own interests.

Time alone is good for planning, organizing, and working on projects you may not get around too otherwise. It can be a very productive time. The biggest problem is deciding which projects to tackle first! Writing this book was in the back of my mind for a long time but I struggled with finding time to write. I finally had to prioritize and let go of other things in order to focus on it.

Do the things you truly enjoy during this time. Make the extra effort to plan, construct, create, or develop whatever it is you feel strongly about.

Take Yourself Out

Initially, this is tough. Going grocery shopping or running errands is one thing but deliberately deciding to go out on your own to a restaurant, concert, or community event is something entirely different. There have been times as an adult when I have felt awkward going places alone. Over the last few years I've developed confidence when it comes to venturing out on my own.

Sometimes people feel uncomfortable going to a movie, restaurant, carnival, fair, museum, etc, by themselves. If those places feel awkward for you, try others you feel better about. It's likely that at first you'll feel uncomfortable with many places you go. Avoid forcing yourself to go places or do things you have no interest in; however, as you move toward change it's helpful to practice being open to new experiences. There is usually a listing of current events in the entertainment section of local papers or online. Also think about treating yourself to something special. What about a massage, manicure, or pedicure? Whatever you decide, be safe while doing so, but take yourself out on a regular basis. Some people who have lived in the same community for many years may have friends and family they can ask out on a regular basis. It's great to have a strong support group but in order to feel comfortable by yourself it helps to go out on your own. One of the reasons we become involved with toxic people is because we aren't comfortable unless we're with others.

I've taken myself out to dinner, movies, museums, bowling, billiards, concerts, sporting events, and community activities. At first, I didn't like going any where people usually gather in pairs or groups but became more comfortable with it as I got used to being in my own company. In the beginning you might find it helpful to keep track of the places you go on a calendar. I did this and was surprised by all my new experiences. Ask yourself: Would any of the people I see when I'm at a restaurant, a concert, or wherever, feel anymore comfortable than I do if they were out alone? We all have times when we're on our own; it's part of life. The more you get out the less difficult it will be. After looking through your local paper, researching online, or finding out about current happenings from another source, pick one or more places you would feel okay going. Once you make the decision don't back down. Go for it and see what happens. You can learn to talk yourself through a variety of situations. Say you go to a café to listen to music. You walk in and there isn't any place to sit down. Don't run for the nearest exit. Take a deep breath, relax, and enjoy the music. If you feel more comfortable go out during daylight hours only. Your safety should always be your first concern.

Volunteer Your Time……Even Just a Little

There are not too many things better in life than reaching out to others. I challenge anyone to feel miserable when they are focused on lending a hand to another person. Life is meant to be shared. We are born into a family and raised in a community. The more time we spend helping others, the less time we spend in isolation; it is healthy for us.

If you're unsure where to start, look in the community section of your local paper. Find an organization that sparks your interest or needs assistance in an area in which you have experience. It is usually a matter of contributing a small amount of time such as an hour per week. If you have children in school, consider helping out in the classroom as a parent volunteer. Serving on budget or planning committees is another great way to give your time and meet others. If you are working a forty hour week it can be a bit more challenging to squeeze in the extra time but it will be worth the effort. Sometimes there are opportunities to do something just one time. There may be a need for adult chaperones at a school function or a community fundraiser. Do you belong to a church, synagogue, or another place of worship? If so, there are usually many volunteer opportunities for one time only events. It doesn't have to be a big commitment on your part. Just giving your time for a little while can make all the difference in the world to you and to others.

Stay in the Moment and Smile

Coming out of a destructive relationship leaves a person drained and not particularly interested in being cheerful and friendly. Give yourself a little time but when you feel like smiling, actually do it! Forget what happened last night. Don't worry about the future. Take a breath, and then take another. Staying in the moment gives you freedom from worry. It allows you to soak in the present. Notice others. You may make someone's day by noticing them. Get used to doing things that are slightly out of your comfort zone. It will help break the pattern of doing things the same old way. You are breaking the mold!

Take Time to Do Nothing

Also allow yourself time to do nothing. This is a busy world. Part of the reason many of us feel overwhelmed is because there are so many things we tell ourselves we need to do and not enough time to do them. Radio, television, and the internet encourage this mindset. We really don't need to be busy doing something every second.

Some of our greatest healing will come in the times when we are doing the simplest of activities or nothing at all.

I read about a man who lived to be 112. It was noted that he ate pancakes and sausage regularly and enjoyed a variety of junk food, however, when an autopsy was done on him, his internal organs were in great shape "clean as a whistle." How could this be when we hear what a big difference a healthy diet plays in living longer?

In this man's case genetics probably played a major

role but not getting caught up in ongoing stress and worry can also make a difference. Life is a balance of good and bad things happening to us. How we deal with the good and the bad has got to factor into how long and how healthful we live. Part of healthy living is learning how to pace ourselves. Being still is good for the mind, body, and spirit.

Have Fun

Having fun makes life worth living. Sure, we work and pay bills to make sure our daily lives run smoothly. We also need to enjoy ourselves!

What you define as fun relates to who you are as a person. Your approach to daily living can help increase the level of enjoyment you have in your life. Even going to your job can be less of a chore and more enjoyable. I often find I'm at my best when I tell myself I'm going to have a good day. Nevertheless, there are times during the work week when I don't want to go. During those times I talk myself through the day. Sometimes, however, I really need a break. Not a major vacation, but time to recharge. When I need the time, I take it. When you hit a rough spot talk yourself through the day. If your circumstances allow it, take a day off to do something special or nothing at all. That may be all it takes to feel refreshed. Create an existence that works for you in all aspects of your life. Do you like your job? Are you comfortable in your home environment? Are there things you can do to change your work and home life that would help you feel more relaxed and lighten your mood? If so, reflect on the changes needed in order to create a happier emotional climate and work on those changes. Something as simple as taking a different route to work can give you a better outlook once you get there. How about a new piece of furniture? Is there a landscaping project you have wanted to tackle? Adding a plant to an open space in or outside your home can add a splash of color and create depth. Have a backyard barbeque. Have friends come over for a game night. We all have the ability to have fun; we just need to explore our options and come up with ideas that fit with who we are.

I love playing catch with my dog. He can catch the ball for about fifteen minutes straight and its fun to count the number of times he retrieves it. This is a simple way to spend my time but I enjoy it and so does my dog! Okay, you're thinking, that's a little boring. Well, it may seem that way at first but I really believe we are all much better off if we learn to appreciate the small things in life. The small moments add up to a pleasant existence.

Discover Your Best Qualities

By discovering what you love about yourself, you will uncover your unique style. Understanding who you are will strengthen your identity, and in turn, increase your self-confidence.

Developing a strong identity increases the likelihood you'll maintain boundaries in your relationships and have a clearer picture of what does and doesn't work for you. You're more likely to confidently tell people what you like and don't like if you've taken the time to figure it out. What makes you stand out from the crowd? Think about it carefully. Many women and men too, are reluctant to consider that they're special because they feel this thinking is egocentric. If taken to the extreme, it could be. Yet for those of us who find ourselves in abusive relationships we often battle low-self esteem because we don't take time to look at our strengths.

This next section will give you an opportunity to zero in on what you love about yourself.

Your Best Qualities

What words describe you? What areas in life do you shine? Are you financially responsible? Do you have an artistic flair? Are you an excellent communicator? You may not be aware of it but you have qualities that others most likely envy.

No Contact

Try this exercise:

What do you believe are your best qualities? What is wonderful about you? This is not the time to look at the negatives. Think about what is truly special about you. To give you a jumpstart, look at the following attributes. Choose 10-20 that are your strongest. Add any that are not listed. Make a copy of this list and post it in a place you will see on a daily basis such as your bathroom mirror, the inside of your closet, next to your bed, or by the kitchen sink. Highlight every quality in a bright color. Read through this list every day to remind yourself what a great person you are! To expand on this list try writing examples of things you have done which relate to a particular quality. For example, if you choose conflict resolver maybe you remember a time your children were arguing and you helped them decide how to take care of the problem without fighting.

THE THINGS I LOVE ABOUT MYSELF

Smart _____ Kind _____ Strong _____
Conflict Resolver _____ Organized _____
Artistic _____ Creative _____ Adaptable _____
Loyal _____ Spiritual _____ Communicator _____
Stylish ___ Responsible _____ Parenting Skills _____
Educated _____ Sense Of Humor _____
Sensitive _____ Caring _____ Philanthropic _____
Brave _____ Exciting _____ Helpful _____

Funny_____   Patient _____   Industrious _____
Generous _____   Ambitious _____   Focused _____
Intellectual _____   Relaxed _____   Passionate _____
Sincere _____   Motivator _____   Enthusiastic_____
Dynamic _____   Musical _____   Intuitive _____
Brave _____   Encouraging _____   Silly _____
Hard Working _____   Lighthearted_____
Calm____   Articulate_____   Compassionate _____

Add any other attributes you would like to list:

Observing Yourself

In addition to determining and frequently reviewing your best qualities, it's a good idea to do some self-observation. Focus on the words you speak when in communication with others.

Say a friend comes up to you and compliments you on the way your hair looks. How are you going to deal with the compliment? In the course of daily conversation we don't have much time to think about how we will respond to something someone says to us in passing. Usually our responses are automatic. However, think briefly about how you might respond to that compliment.

Would you thank the person? Would you make eye contact while thanking them? Would you quickly change the subject once the compliment is given?

No Contact

Or would you say something to the effect of; "Oh, I don't know, I think it's too long" or short or whatever the case may be? Remember that a compliment is a gift and when we accept it graciously, the sender feels good in addition to it making our day.

We all communicate with a variety of people on any given day. These people include friends, family, and co-workers. In the past I didn't pay too much attention to how I felt in response to a question asked or a direction given. Now I take more time and think about it. I still respond but pay more attention to what I think and feel first. I don't worry about the silence between the question and my response. I'm more willing to let the question hang a little while in order to give a thoughtful reply.

Do you take a little time before you respond to someone or do you respond quickly to prevent a pause of silence? There is nothing wrong with a pause. If the other person is in a hurry, they will most likely tell you, and catch up with you at a later time. Many people worry about how they come off when in conversation with another person. Do your best to relax and communicate respectfully with other people but don't stress out over everything you say. Be patient with yourself and the other person and good communication will follow.

Essentially, if we take more time with ourselves, we are less likely to have conversations with abusers and in turn develop relationships with them. An abuser is usually not a patient person. Some abusers like to control conversations. When you first meet one they may show you quite a bit of attention, maybe even hang on your every word. It doesn't take long though to notice that they lose interest in conversations you have with them. Be alert and look for clues when getting to know a new person. Do they look at you when you speak? Is their a nice flow to the conversation? Do they usually follow and show an interest in the conversation, or do they seem distracted and uninterested? Are they frequently irritated or easily take offense in conversations with you? Do you feel comfortable when in conversation with them? Eventually, if you're talking with an abuser, you will notice the impatience, lack of interest, or another clue, and will decide this isn't someone you want further contact with. Remember to pay attention to what you are thinking feeling and observing. You end up saving yourself much time (maybe even a lifetime) of wasted effort.

Chapter 5
Processing the Loss and Making Changes

Back Flashes

You will notice times when you remember conversations or events you shared with your ex. Processing these memories instead of trying to ignore or push them away to the back of your mind is part of your healing. Sometimes we push the memories aside because it's too painful to remember. Process the memories because if you don't the end result may be a new relationship with another abuser.

In the early days after leaving the last relationship I often went over conversations I had with him. One conversation had to do with him telling me not to express any sadness regarding the relationship and also not to express any feelings of love toward him. There were times when he would look me straight in the eye and tell me that he would leave if I continued to talk about my feelings.....

Another memory was from a year into the relationship: One evening I made a comment about us as a couple. He thought it was amusing I would consider us a couple. I remember him saying: "You and me? You actually think of us as a couple?" He laughed. At the time I thought, is there a joke here I'm missing? Is there a punch line I don't get? I didn't realize it at the time but he wanted me to see that a fullfledged relationship with him was out of my reach.

I needed to relive this conversation many times in order to understand the meaning it had for me. It was actually devastating at the time but instead of expressing my heartbreak in the moment, I ignored my feelings and continued on with the relationship determined to convince him I was good enough. *What I realized later that I didn't process in the actual conversation:*

You're not the man I want.
I have value and you don't seem to see it.
Said goodbye
Made my exit and never look back.

Process the memories. You may have some of those ah-ha moments. To me these are great moments because they bring satisfaction and a sense of accomplishment. You figured something out you may have been struggling to understand for quite some time. These moments will help you see this person in a different light. You may be able to look back and think-- why didn't I see this before?

In my example from above, I noticed and felt hurt by his remark as soon as he made it but it took me more time to process through the conversation. I had to wait until I was ready to examine the pain associated with the remark since I refused to face it during the actual conversation. When you pay attention and trust your instincts in the moment, you end up getting out of bad situations sooner. When you process your feelings and trust your instincts you'll make decisions which are right for you.

I Heard That Song and It Reminded Me of...

You may hear a particular song or remember certain moments and become sentimental. This is natural. You're remembering a person you shared your life with. If you become teary let it happen and realize it will pass.

As time goes by you will develop a natural distance between yourself and this person. It won't happen over night but it will happen. Remember, you have control over your emotions. They don't control you! If the emotion comes out it is up to you to work through it. Think of these emotions as if they were little viruses. If you're resistance is weak, they can take over. Don't let them! Gently move them out of your consciousness. Feel them if you need to, then let them go.

As Time Passes

You will feel differently after each day, week, month, and year, you no longer have contact, or if necessary, only minimal contact. At first it will take a great deal of effort to get through each hour day and week. Getting through the first month will be a huge milestone. The urges to make contact will lessen over time.

It won't be long before you feel relief living without the extreme highs and lows you got used to experiencing. It's exhausting to live like that and will feel as if a tremendous load has been lifted when you no longer have the constant strain. There will also be a new sense of joy in your life. Simple plans take on new meaning because you're making them rather than waiting for someone else to.

Observing Other People

I have found it valuable to observe others: co-workers, clients, friends, family members, strangers, even people on television. Subconsciously, we are observing others every day, however, to deliberately observe people is a little different. When observing others I don't mean that you're attempting to judge the character of a stranger—save that for super-sleuths with training. What I'm talking about here is seeking opportunities to observe others who do a good job holding a conversation.

You might also try observing how people react to disappointment, or how people say "no" to someone.

I find it useful to watch certain characters on soap operas. In soap opera land, characters are very direct in their dealings with others (though I'm not saying they don't keep secrets because secrets keep these stories on the air). However, the characters are not afraid if they offend someone else. That is what makes the story lines interesting to watch. Often these characters do and say things we wouldn't in real life. It is also interesting to observe people who are in some type of competition to see how they hold up under pressure. I find the TV show, American Idol, to be fascinating in this way. The contestants sing before judges, the studio audience, and millions at home and do surprisingly well holding up under such intense pressure. I sometimes visualize myself in a public speaking situation I'm fearful of and compare it to what any of those contestants are experiencing and it doesn't seem quite so bad.

Observation Assignment

Observe women who don't communicate well with their partner, child, friend, or parent. What type of attitude do they exhibit? What do they do that hurts their communication?
Study what they do. Then: **Avoid communicating in that manner.**
Where to find these people: Stores, restaurants, parks, malls, any public place where there are groups of people.

Next, observe women who seem to have the attention of the person they are in conversation with. What sets them apart from others? What do they do and say that brings respect? Do they appear confident? What is their conversation style?
Pay attention and then: **Practice a similar style for yourself.**

The point is, you can learn a lot by observing people in a variety of settings and studying their reactions. If you have been in a relationship with a controlling or domineering person you may not be practiced in noticing what you think about a lot of things. Observing others in a variety of circumstances allows you to think about your reactions in situations you might encounter in your own life. If you see communication that impresses you in a positive way you can take note of it for future reference. Sometimes I observe couples and notice how the women behave around their partners. I watch their mannerisms and listen to the inflection in their voices when they speak to them. I notice women who seem to have confidence in their ability to communicate with men and those who seem more self-conscious. I observe the reactions of the men these women are with. Which men seem the most attentive? Which women seem to expect the respect of the men they are with? How do they do it? Observe the various styles of communication. Do you see styles that remind you of your own or of how you would like to communicate in the future?

Some women regularly apologize. They apologize even when they said nothing that would indicate an apology was necessary and seem to do it out of habit. Maybe they want to avoid conflict or want to please others.

We're all capable of effective communication; sometimes the problem is just not having enough practice. The more skilled we are at communicating, the easier it will be to develop confidence in situations which normally cause anxiety, such as speaking to an authority figure, confrontation, or meeting new people.

Good communication requires a high level of self-awareness. Understanding your own personal style of communicating will help you create positive and lasting impressions on others. There are many books available on communication. Two I believe would prove valuable are <u>I Know I'm In There Somewhere</u> by Helene Brenner, PhD and <u>Messages</u> by Matthew

McKay, Martha Davis, and Patrick Fanning.

Listening Assignment

Listen to a friend and during your conversation pay attention to exactly what this person is saying.

While listening be centered. Be open to hearing what they have to say.
Give your friend your total attention and let them know they have it. Avoid distractions.
Look at them while they're speaking. If you don't understand something, ask for clarification.
Use your intuition while they are speaking. Listen for what is said as well as what is not said. How do you feel when they are speaking? If something doesn't seem right ask for clarification.
Don't interrupt as it sends a message that what you say is more important than what they say.
Be patient.
Keep your emotions in check.

There are times, especially when we're nervous, that we hear the words of another person but aren't really listening. Instead, we're thinking about what we will say in response to what they've just said. Much of the actual content of the conversation escapes us because we've got this side talk going on in our minds where we're criticizing, judging, or evaluating ourselves. When we lack confidence we put too much emphasis on our own inhibitions.

Practice the above assignment and listen with genuine interest to what the other person is saying. Also watch your emotional involvement in the conversation as it could be distracting. You will have a difficult time paying attention if you are emotionally involved and may miss some of what is said. After the conversation, think about how they react to your efforts? How does it make you feel to carefully listen? Really listening to another person is a gift to us and the other person. We all need to be heard and understood.

Think about the Role You Played

Make it a goal to be honest with yourself regarding the role you played in the relationship. If you face the role you played you decrease the chances of playing the same role again.

While in several past relationships, I often played the role of the deaf dumb and blind girlfriend. I didn't hear what was said if it wasn't what I wanted to hear. I often didn't tell others what was going on because I wanted to think I had it all under control. I was blind when it came to seeing the role I played in keeping these relationships status quo. Here is one experience:

There were a handful of times when I suspected one partner took things from me however I never had proof. One time in particular, I went to the store and brought home household supplies. Among these supplies was a pack of light bulbs. I brought the bag with the supplies in the house and set it on the kitchen table. I could see the pack of light bulbs inside the bag. Later that evening, my boyfriend came to visit...

The next morning I went to take the supplies out of the bag and noticed the light bulbs weren't there. I asked my sons if they had taken them out and they said no. I knew I hadn't touched the bag because I had planned on emptying it at a later time. The only other person in the house the night before was my friend. The next time he came over I confronted him about it. He denied taking them and thought it was funny I was even concerned about light bulbs. Because of his remarks, I dropped the subject for a few weeks though the disappearance continued to bother me. The next time I brought it up I told him I believed he took them. Again he denied it but I watched him carefully and observed his back stiffen and shoulders straighten. Hmm, I thought to myself, he's lying.

Never-the-less, I continued on in the relationship. I rationalized that I was making a big deal out of nothing and still had no proof he took them. I did have my instincts though, and refused to follow them.

No Contact

Always follow your instincts; they will not steer you wrong. What I should have done when I was suspicious:

Trusted my instincts
Ended the relationship
Never look back

If like me, you've played the role of being deaf dumb and blind, accept that you went along with lies and/or half-truths, and not following your instincts. My focus was how do I keep this thing going instead of how do I get the heck out! I was determined to hold onto the relationship and keep the peace by looking the other way. If you have a tendency toward peace at any price, work toward eliminating this way of thinking. The next section discusses red flags.

I Will Never Choose This Again!
Avoid Becoming a Target

Deciding not to ever go through this again, was one of my first thoughts after leaving the last relationship. However, just making that decision wasn't enough. I had to make a daily effort to pay attention to what others say and what I think about what they say. It's not enough to say "I will never get involved with a disordered person again" or "I will never choose to be a victim again."

Paying attention isn't going to totally eliminate mistakes but it reduces the likelihood of needing no contact in the future.

Also, pay attention to your **Red Flags** in order to avoid having to get to this place again. Don't ignore them; they are there to help you.

What Are Red Flags?

Red flags are possible relationship warning signs. Not necessarily bad, but a signal to investigate further for underlying problems not previously recognized. Keep in mind that there may be extenuating circumstances for any of them, so interpret them in context.

- Smells like liquor drugs or tobacco
- Rude to others
- Lets you do all the talking
- Cruel to animals
- Lies, cheats, steals
- Jealous, possessive
- Doesn't like children
- Falls in love quickly
- Turns hot and cold (moody)
- Emotional extremes
- No regard for laws, rules, etiquette
- Doesn't share thoughts readily
- Is wishy-washy, noncommittal
- Uncomfortable with emotions
- Secretive, defensive

No Contact

- Exhibits little emotion (flat affect)
- Critical of self and others
- Blames others for problems
- Overly concerned with appearance
- Selfish or greedy
- Doesn't reveal much about himself/activities
- Poor loser
- Won't take you to his/her home
- Lazy or irresponsible
- Poor listener
- Controlling or demanding
- Drives recklessly
- Shy/withdrawn
- Does not have an income
- Disrespectful or abusive
- Poor personal hygiene
- Sloppy dresser
- Financially irresponsible
- Complains frequently
- No or low motivation
- Lacks confidence
- No goals
- No friend or family contacts
- Pushes physical relationship quickly
- Excessive name calling, "idiots" etc.
- Does all the talking
- Lacks empathy for others

This list isn't all-inclusive. There may be other red flags you wish to add. Also, if any of these apply to you, consider them as possible goals for change. It could be that some of the above red flags seem normal because you have accepted them in others for so long. You may have also taken on some of these characteristics in order to stay in a relationship with an abuser.

Reflections

By this time, you have done a lot of work. You may have left or are leaving a destructive path and are beginning your journey on a new one full of possibilities.

Review what you have learned and stay focused on your resolve to maintain no or limited contact.

Keep monitoring your progress and resolve because you learn better when you hold yourself accountable. You're also less likely to slip back into old patterns.

Chapter 6
You're Unique!

Believe in Yourself

The old adage is that a strong defense makes a good offense. You're not likely to believe you will fail if you consider yourself a winner. Believing in you will bring positive results.

Some of us make the mistake of wanting things to happen too quickly whether it is in a relationship, career move, making a major purchase, home improvement project etc. The problem is we hate waiting. We want everything to have already happened and waiting for the change makes us anxious. We feel what we want is never going to happen so get antsy and attempt to make things happen as quickly as possible.

Why?

Maybe we look around and see others who have what we want. When not in a relationship we might think "What's wrong with me? Other people have this, why don't I?" So we decide to speed things up.

We hurry things up at work, school, home out of fear we'll be stuck forever.

A home improvement project might not get the desired results because the job was done too quickly. Look at it this way, if you stick with the project, it will get done. You'll also have a great feeling of accomplishment to go along with the improvement.

Continue to believe in yourself and good things will come your way. If you've got a good sense of who you are you're not going to be easily swayed or confused by pressure from other people. The same goes with relationships. Take your time and focus on knowing who you are and what you really want. Allow some room for flexibility because if you're used to a certain type of person you'll subconsciously seek that type even if it's not the best one for you. The more time you take to get to know yourself the more likely you'll be to find healthy people you feel comfortable with.

You Are the Authority on You

You live with yourself day in and day out. You know your thoughts, words, and actions. Do you believe you know yourself? Do you know yourself based on who others think you are or by whom you think you are?

We spend our lives listening to other people. From the moment we enter this world we're learning about ourselves through the eyes of others. If we are lucky, we will hear more positive things than negative ones. Young children are impressionable and view themselves the way the significant people in their lives view them.

For example, a young child may grow and learn that he is smart, strong, and makes good decisions. He has a little brother who isn't quite so lucky. The little brother may hear he's not as smart or as strong as his brother. He may also hear he doesn't catch a ball as well or doesn't read as well etc. as his older brother.

All of our young lives we hear all about ourselves from others, primarily our parents. As we get older we form our own opinions about who we are. The challenge is to balance the information we hear from others regarding who we are, with what we learn from our own unique experiences.

There are people we form relationships with who are eager to let us know what they think of us. Unfortunately, some of these people do not have our best interests at heart. They want us to believe we are less than who we really are. It makes them feel better about themselves if they can make us feel inferior.

No matter how much you may admire, respect, and trust another person, remember, they don't know you as well as you know yourself. What others think about you is their opinion. Listen to and reflect on what they say but be cautious about accepting what others say in regards to defining who you are as an individual.

You have the responsibility of believing in yourself. You will want and at times need advice from others but trust your own thinking. If you're not sure about a decision run it by a trusted friend or relative however, remember, you have a mind to use and instincts to guide you through decision making. Pay attention to your instincts. As you learn to follow them you'll gain confidence in your ability to make good choices.

You Know What You Are Thinking

There are times when we don't believe we are thinking clearly about a variety of things. This may be a result of not making enough choices early in life or because others have regularly questioned the choices we have made. Whatever the reason, the result is we don't trust our own thinking. Sometimes even when we make a decision, if it's not what another person tells us they would choose we think our decision is wrong. Our decision making process is unique to us and our situation. It doesn't make our decision a bad one if another person or ten people wouldn't make the same choice—it just means our decision is different from what someone else might choose based on multiple factors. If we take time to think through our decisions, research when needed, and if we want—seek opinions from those we trust, there's no reason to believe our decisions aren't sound. We can always make adjustments or start over. If another person tells you that you don't know what you're thinking or that you aren't thinking clearly don't immediately discount your thought process. Here is an example from my personal experience:

I had wanted to get a dog. My last dog died four years earlier. I felt I was ready for another one but a friend said, "you don't want a dog; a dog is a bad idea." His concern was a surprise to me since he had a dog and seemed to enjoy having one... I gave up on the idea for a while then came back to it again. For the next few months I continued to go back and forth. I knew I wanted a dog but instead of going with my own thoughts, paid more attention to what someone else told me I should do.

Eventually, I did enough self talk, was convinced my thinking was fine, and was clear about my decision. My children wanted a dog and so did I regardless of what anyone else thought; so at last we got one. After having the puppy for several weeks my friend still tried to convince me I should give the dog up because he would be too much trouble. As it turned out, we kept the dog and have never regretted that decision.

Trust your thinking when it comes to ideas and decisions. If you want a second opinion run it by someone you trust but face that they may not see things the way you do. If they don't it doesn't mean you should immediately jump ship with your own thinking. You have a mind to use and instincts to help guide you through decision making. Listen to others because there are things they might see that you haven't considered. However, pay attention to your instincts because by following them, you will gain confidence in your ability to make good choices.

Your Opinion Matters

If you continue to maintain contact with an abuser remind yourself that your opinions matter and you have value. A big reason for leaving a narcissist and maintaining no contact is because these people just suck the life out of those they are close to. They come across as being superior but secretly know they're not. Sometimes they're happy; sometimes they're sad just like everyone else but they don't have well-developed personalities. They want what they want when they want it. They use other people and feed off the attention they receive in order to feel in control. In order to be around one of them you've got to go along with their game plan. If they are having a good day they want you to be on board with them. If they're having a bad day, they expect you will either stay out of their way or stay in that bad place right along with them. If on the other hand, you are having a bad day; it's not likely they will deal well with it as it's difficult for them to cope with the emotional ups and downs of others.

Being in a relationship with a narcissist/abuser is confusing because they present well. They appear charming, intelligent, and confident. They're also opinionated and initially seem sincere and genuine. In addition, what they have to say sounds rational and well thought out. However, when you dig a little deeper, or observe how they live their lives, their words and actions don't match. Often individuals who lack confidence gravitate toward narcissists and other abusers. This happens because we get sucked in by the charm and forget to pay attention to what is going on. Abusers are often adept at distracting others; they know what they're doing. Over time, we may even start to believe our opinions are the same as theirs even if that's not the case. It doesn't take long before we're really not sure what we think about a lot of things.

Pay attention to what your mind and body are telling you when in conversation with other people. After leaving a relationship with an abuser, if you're patient you'll begin to trust your opinions again and offer them to others. An opinion is a judgment, belief, attitude, or a personal view. Whoever is stating an opinion owns the words they are speaking. It is up to the person listening to determine what they think about what is being said. Don't buy stock in another person's words just as they shouldn't buy stock in yours.

Who Am I?

This is a question we spend most of our lives trying to answer. We find out new things about ourselves every day. Getting up each morning should be a wonderful opportunity for new experiences and to learn more about the world around us. The more positive the approach we take in our lives the more we will appreciate what each day has to offer.

Take a walk at sunrise, spend time with people who admire and love you. Pick yourself some flowers or buy a bouquet. The joy you give to yourself is equal to that you can get from another person. Think about all you have accomplished and plan to accomplish in the future. Give yourself a hug *or* get yourself a little chocolate. I've heard that eating chocolate actually starts the same chemical reaction in your brain as getting hugged! Whatever you do remind yourself how special you are. You are a person who has decided to take back your life and enjoy it!

This Is What I Look Like

In order to get a clear picture of what you look like, you need to look at yourself and then write down a description. What color are your hair skin and eyes? How tall are you? What is your body type? What are your best features? Look at your face and describe what you see. Concentrate on the positives. Many of us only see the deficiencies. We don't see our attractiveness. Focus on the positive.

Exercise: List ten or more things about your appearance you like. After completing this list post it somewhere. To expand on this idea, take a picture of yourself, mount it on tag board, and attach your list. If you want, frame the picture and list. Have fun and be creative with this. Just remember to place your picture in a place you will see on a regular basis.

If *you* believe there are things you could do to make yourself more attractive, such as changing a hairstyle, making healthier food choices, exercising, or reducing stress, make those changes. Incorporate fruits and vegetables into your diet and drink water. Avoid a high consumption of sugar as it can lead to premature aging. It can also suppress the immune system. Cut back on your alcohol intake and cigarette smoking if you smoke. Once you have made the changes you want to make focus on making your life better by learning as much as you can and enjoying yourself. At the end of your life, those you have touched will remember you because of the way you made them feel, not because of how you looked.

Your Interests and Passions

If there is something you have always wanted to do, now is a great time to give it a try. You may not be able to quit your job to follow your dream, but you can work on it a little at a time. What are you passionate about? What do you like to do in your free time? Is there a potential hobby or even an income possibility?

When I was in my twenties I wanted to have my own business: I tried building a hot dog cart, had a home sewing business, and wrote articles for a local publication. My objective at the time was to bring some income into the household while staying home and raising my children. I was excited about pursuing these businesses but didn't have support

No Contact

from my spouse. He felt these businesses didn't bring in enough income to merit the effort. The income was definitely small in the beginning but there was potential for more and I had a strong desire to contribute financially to the household. However, without encouragement from my spouse, I became discouraged so didn't give any of the businesses enough time to develop.

If you are leaving a destructive relationship and money is not an issue you may be able to pursue a hobby as an income producing venture. If, on the other hand, you need a steady income and don't have the extra funds to pour into a business, you may need to work full time and fit your hobby in during your off hours. Just don't give up on it! Give yourself the okay to pursue a strong interest. If you have something you love doing it gets you excited and takes priority on your list of things to do, pay attention to that! It can be anything and it doesn't have to be a money earning venture. If *you* value and love doing it, it's worthwhile. My dad was a stamp and coin collector. He started collecting stamps when he was 13 years old. He continued it right up until his death. He taught the young and old about his hobby. He displayed his stamps at post offices and libraries throughout the local area. He also offered workshops at local schools demonstrating and teaching children stamp collecting basics. I think there are at least a few children who became excited about stamp collecting largely because he introduced them to the hobby.

Brainstorm and list ten or more things you love doing or would like to get more information about. Don't spend too much time thinking about what to put on the list. Write down ten things that first come to mind.

Check List

1._____

2._____

3._____

4._____

5._____

6._____

7._____

8._____

9._____

10._____

Now that you have your list, look it over. Are there any interests that jump out at you? Could any have income earning potential? Are there any you've put on the back burner and said to yourself, "some day I will do this?" If so, is there a small first step you could take to make it happen?

A next step might be to look at the interests in order of their appeal to you. Once you discover which one is the most appealing, no matter what it is, take action to get more information. If your idea requires additional knowledge go online or to your local library. Get as much information as you can. Discipline yourself and work on it a little at a time. If this is something you have a strong interest in, you may discover you're willing to take the time and make the effort to pursue it. However, if you find that although the idea sounds appealing, there are too many barriers in the way, you will have your answer. Don't dismiss an idea too soon because you may see something as a barrier that really isn't. Say you're interested in starting your own business but don't have start up funds, is that really a barrier? Have you researched possible funding sources? Check out all possibilities. If you find you are losing enthusiasm the more you research one of your choices, it may be an indication you aren't as interested as you thought. Keep this up until you find something you want to pursue. If nothing on your list really captures your attention, start another list. It may surprise you to discover that your initial brainstorming doesn't bring up any serious possibilities. Continue the brainstorming process without judging your choices and the ideas will start flow-ing. Stick with the process until you find an idea you keep coming back to and really want to get more information about.

Checking in on the No Contact

Have you maintained no contact? If contact is necessary due to co-parenting responsibilities have you kept the contact to a minimum, having only the most necessary type which involves children and/or scheduling concerns?

How are you feeling? Chances are if you are beginning to feel better about your life and future, it's because you have consistently maintained no contact, or if you have children, have kept only minimal contact regarding parenting, school, and activity scheduling. Having control over your own life and being responsible for your decisions will give you a new perspective regarding the options available to you.

On the other hand, if you have slipped and abandoned no contact or have not followed through with minimum contact don't panic! There are no penalties for having slipped. You will most likely feel frustration about continuing or restarting the communication but you can always start the no contact process again. You are the only one who can decide if you are ready and willing to commit to it. If you aren't ready, reading this book may still give you good information in order to make healthier decisions regarding the direction you want to take and the manner in which you relate to your partner or ex-partner. You may want to reread certain sections again. This book can be used as a tool and will still be available if and when you decide you are ready to move forward with no contact.

Many people who have been in destructive relationships find that it takes more than one effort to break it off. It can take several or more attempts before finally deciding you do not want to go back to the relationship. Chapter 9 discusses relapsing.

Chapter 7
Listening to Yourself

Journaling

This should be fun and not a chore. If it becomes something you dread you won't do it. Some people are comfortable using a spiral notebook. Others prefer a hardbound or leather bound book specifically for journaling which can be bought at a bookstore. Use what you enjoy handling. Look at the texture of the cover. Maybe you want to make a book cover out of a favorite fabric. The key is to make it a book that is durable and one you will look forward to using.

There is also no set length when writing your entries though it may help to have the goal of writing at least one paragraph for each entry. There have been days when I have entered two or three pages and other days when I entered just a few words. Write as much or as little as you feel like writing. Use writing tools you enjoy using. Pencils, pens, markers, it really makes no difference as long as you are comfortable and have fun with the tools you use.

Secondly, it is a good idea to date your entries because then you can revisit your thoughts from the past. You'll also see the growth you have made over time. There may be thoughts you have or events you describe that you want to refer to at a later time. Dating your entries is an excellent way to track your writing.

Journaling about Career Changes

After my marriage ended I went to a local workshop entitled <u>Restoring Career Opportunities: Thinking Critically about Domestic Violence</u>. A major part of this workshop had to do with journaling. Each week during this four week workshop there was a journal assignment. One of the assignments had to do with how my expectations or feelings about pursuing an occupation were influenced by others' expectations. I was to think about specific people in my life and their expectations of me. I found this assignment helpful as I had been strongly influenced by others. You are going through many changes. If you are thinking about a new career or change in career please answer the following questions:

What are your expectations about pursuing or succeeding in any one occupational, career, or educational area?

Are your expectations or feelings about pursuing an occupation influenced by others' expectations of you? How? Think about specific people in your life and their expectations of you.

How are you affected by others' encouragement or discouragement (how do you feel, what do you think, what do you do, when you hear encouragement or discouragement)?

Answering the above questions can help you determine where your motivation toward specific career goals is coming from. It may also offer some insight regarding how much you are influenced by the views of other people in other areas of your life.

Be Honest with Yourself When You Write

Always be honest with yourself in your writing. No one else needs to read what you've written. It's for you. Write freely and truthfully. You will look back and see your thought processes at each stage of your healing. Note all that you have learned and discovered. If there are decisions you are struggling with, writing them down as you work through them is often a way to bring clarity. Documenting your changes is a way to stay focused on your healing and measure the growth you've achieved.

Sometimes Keeping Your Hopes and Dreams to Yourself Is a Good Idea

Have you ever had a great idea you couldn't wait to share, but then when you do, get the feeling it didn't go over so well? Have you shared plans for school, a new job, or business idea, only to be told that school just isn't for you, the new job isn't a good fit, or that your business idea sounds good but it's too much work or is too expensive?

Sometimes it can be a good idea to keep our dreams to ourselves. If we keep ideas to ourselves temporarily, it gives us the opportunity to let them simmer. Then when we're confident, we can share our plans with those we trust.

When I was nearing the seventh month of a yearlong divorce process I decided I wanted to build a house. I would look out my kitchen window and see a new housing development going up. I didn't know how in the world I was going to buy a lot in that development let alone build a house but knew that's what I wanted to do. As it turned out, I found a realtor who sug-

No Contact

gested I speak with a local contractor he knew. The contractor ended up purchasing the land and building the house for me. I chose a house plan, submitted it to him, and he built it. I secured a home loan and purchased the house once it was completed. It all worked out beautifully and my sons and I had a brand new home to live in!

It took me awhile to share the house building project with anyone else. I thought I might become discouraged by another person's remarks because I was at such a vulnerable point in my life. I wasn't used to choosing a contractor and overseeing a building project by myself. I was also on a tight budget scrimping and saving for the necessary funds. In addition, I feared that in one way or another, things wouldn't work out. By keeping my plan to myself I stayed focused each day as I saw forward progress being made. As the days went by and the building progressed I became more confident that my children and I would actually live in the house. I also felt more comfortable sharing my housing project with close friends and family. It was exciting to see the look on their faces when I told them that my dream was becoming a reality.

Three-time Olympic 100 m champion athlete, Gail Devers says:
Keep your dreams alive. Understand to achieve anything requires faith and belief in yourself, vision, hard work, determination, and dedication.

Daydreaming Can Be Very Healthy and Enlightening

Psychologists estimate that we daydream for one-third to one-half of our waking hours, although a single daydream only lasts a few minutes.

Daydreaming is often thought of as a waste of time and that it interferes with productivity. Daydreams can be a problem if they cause you to lose focus and forget information. On the other hand, daydreams can boost productivity. Say you're working on a project and your mind wanders. You won't be productive if you're losing focus or are tired. Lean back and close your eyes. Let your mind wander to your heart's content for ten minutes or so. Imagine about things, places, and people. Think about an issue you have been struggling with. While relaxing, you may find a solution or at least a different way of looking at the issue. When your break time is up chances are you will feel refreshed, in a better mood, and ready to get things done!

At a time when you are making life changing decisions, daydreams can be especially helpful because they give you the opportunity to sort through decisions you must make and issues you face.

Daydreaming can also be of great benefit to you as you heal and grow. It can be a tool in your arsenal. Just remember that it is useful when used wisely and for short periods of time.

Listening to Yourself as You Talk to Others

In Chapter 4 you looked at monitoring your involvement when in conversation with others. The focus was on how you feel and respond during conversations. This section is a little different. Have you ever listened to yourself while you are talking to someone else? Have you focused on the words coming out of your mouth? It isn't easy to do. I find that when I'm listening to my own words it's harder to focus on the actual conversation. Nevertheless, listening to yourself gives you a much better idea of what the other person hears when they are listening to you.

Listen to the sound of your voice. Do you like it?

How fast do you speak? Are you quick? Hurried? Slow? Deliberate? Do your words stumble over each other with enthusiasm?

How about your tone of voice: Are you soft-spoken? Do you have a gentle voice? Are you boisterous?

Does your voice change in new situations?
I've noticed times when I need to clear my throat before speaking. I used to think I had some ongoing throat condition but after talking with my doctor

found out that the throat is full of tiny nerve endings which are sensitive to anxiety and stress. That seemed to make sense as I only seemed to have the problem when I was anxious or nervous.

Exercise: Have a conversation with someone. If there are no available humans at the moment, wait until you have one around. It doesn't count if you talk to yourself. You must be able to make eye contact with another person. This doesn't need to be a long conversation; one to five minutes will work.

The objective is to listen to the sound of your voice to see how it makes you feel. Do you like the tone? Does the volume seem about right? If you adjust the volume of your voice will you sound more confident? Often when we're in an abusive relationship, we don't have a lot of confidence when we speak. Maybe we get used to being ignored so stop contributing to conversations. As a result, our voices become softer. What you say is important, you just need to believe in the value of your words and let that come through when you speak. In the above exercise focus on your words and the information you're trying to get across. After the exchange, think about the conversation. Did you like the sound of your voice? Were you able to get your point across? Was the other person attentive while you spoke? Were you attentive to the other person when it was their turn to speak? Were you distracted during the conversation? Did you look around the room or in some other way not pay attention? Were you calm or nervous during the exchange? How fast or slow did you speak?

The style we use when we communicate with others might seem like a small issue but it isn't. We need to pay attention to it because we're often judged not so much by what we say, but by how we say it. People notice those who come across as hesitant or unsure of themselves in social situations. More aggressive types might see those who come off as hesitant and unsure as easy marks. If we consistently choose to spend time with people who don't give us their full attention, ignore us, or interrupt us when we speak, we sell ourselves short.

Present yourself as being confident when you speak, even if you're not, and you will get respect. Stay humble and let your warmth shine through. When you respect yourself you will seek people who show respect for others.

Also think about eye contact. Most North Americans, especially Caucasians, prefer to have a lot of eye contact when they talk to another person. However many shy people make very little or no eye contact. They tend to look down or away instead of looking at their conversation partner's face. It isn't necessary to stare at the other person while speaking to them but an occasional friendly gaze lets them know you're participating in the conversation.

There are people who do stare too intently into the other person's eyes which usually makes the conversation partner feel uncomfortable. Some people use this tactic to intimidate; however many people who do this are not aware they're creating a negative impression. When speaking with another person, smile, nod, and gaze at the entire face as well as the eyes. Also glance away for brief periods. The idea is to keep you as at ease as the person you're speaking to.

It isn't always easy to stay engaged during conversations because there usually are distractions. However, if you glance around the room too much, or frequently look at other people, your conversation partner may think you're bored, or that you are looking around for someone else you'd rather talk to. You want their attention and vice versa.

Pay attention to detail in your conversations. What do you do that keeps you and the other person engaged? What do other people do while listening and talking to you? Look for patterns. If you think there are things you can do to improve your conversations concentrate on making those changes.

Do I Always Have to Agree with Others?

No! And if disagreeing is especially hard for you, you should make a point of doing it more often! If

No Contact

you always agree with everything others say you're either not being honest with yourself or don't have any opinions. As was stated previously, some people who have been in abusive relationships don't regularly state their views or give opinions.

It can be nicer to agree with what someone else says as it may make a relationship go smoother but if in truth you don't agree with what is said you're lying to yourself and the other person. Take the risk and say no when you mean no. A parent doesn't have too much trouble telling a two year old child not to run out in the middle of the street or not to pull another child's hair. The two year old may cry but running in the street or hair pulling can't go on. It's different however when dealing with a coworker, parent, significant other, or spouse. We tend to look at possible outcomes before responding negatively. Will it mean I won't get the promotion if I say no to the boss's request? Will my mother stop calling if I tell her I don't want to come to dinner on Sunday? Will my spouse go without me if I tell him I don't want to go on vacation right now?

Some women continue to stay in destructive relationships because they're indecisive. Their partners assume the relationship is fine because these women never say anything. Eventually, some will decide they do want out and tell their partners they want to end the relationship, but then aren't firm in their resolve. In other words, they say they want to leave but continue to stay.

There is nothing wrong with being in agreement with others or changing your mind if a decision you've made doesn't feel right. However, there is something wrong if you never disagree, don't honestly state your opinions, and typically don't follow through once you've made a decision. Avoid getting hung up on outcomes. If you do, you will likely be stuck in relationships you don't want with people who aren't good for you. It is a risk to tell another person "no" or disagree with someone you care about. However, in the long run, you will resent any person you feel you have to agree with in order to keep in your life. Look at it this way, by disagreeing with another person you allow them the freedom to disagree with you! All of us should be honest about who we are when interacting with others. If our disagreeing causes them to discontinue a connection with us then we just found something out: we crossed one of their boundaries. Our opinion was one they couldn't live with and when that's the case it's best to let go of the connection gracefully.

You Are Changing Your Thought Patterns

The self talk that goes on in our minds has to do with what we feel, think, and want, what others would like, what is expected, as well as what we're capable of. All of these thoughts can be different.

No Contact

You may hear others tell you "you're no good at this or that" and you start to believe it. These thoughts become incorporated into your self talk.

Negative thoughts go hand in hand with destructive relationships. It is hard to have anything but negative thoughts running through your mind when you face daily put downs and discouragement. These thoughts don't go away just because this person is no longer in your life. It will take a conscious effort to keep from hitting rewind.

In Chapter 4 you looked at discovering your best qualities. You chose 10 to 20 of those listed and/or added some of your own. Did you post your list? Do you look at it daily? An excellent way to change negative thoughts is to remind yourself daily about your best qualities. If you truly believe you have these qualities keep them in the forefront. It's easy to complete any exercise one time. It's harder to think about your positive attributes regularly. One way to do it is to have visual reminders. Posting your list of attributes will be a reminder of your strengths. If you want to post it in a private spot, great! Just make sure you give yourself the opportunity to look at it on a regular basis. Posting it in a prominent place for all to see is even better!

Another way to work on negative thoughts is to be aware when you're having them. Say you make a mistake on a project at work or home and tell yourself you're stupid. Pause after that thought. Tell yourself you really don't believe you're stupid, you just made a mistake. Turn it around by saying "I'm smart and capable." Always remember to treat yourself well; you'll feel better and respect yourself more.

Chapter 8
But I Still Care about This Person

Do You Care about the Person or the Dream?

Most likely you have conflicting feelings about your ex partner. You may have left and maintained no contact, but still hold out for change. You want to believe they will come back ready to compromise and in addition, willing to get the help it will take to be in a healthy relationship. Of course the possibility exists that this will happen although it isn't probable. It's more likely they will attempt to contact you and if they succeed will be quite amicable. However, if you were to return to the relationship, you would likely see the changes don't last. In fact, a return could result in an escalation of abuse.

Leaving a relationship is a process. Ending a relationship with an abuser is one of the hardest things you will ever do. The relationship is bad because it is one that causes continual frustration. There is potential but that potential is always just out of reach for a variety of reasons. Maybe they're attached to someone else, maybe they don't want a committed relationship, or aren't capable of one. The relationship was bad because it lacked what one or both people needed. You may continue to care about this person from a distance; but to stay in a relationship with someone who either doesn't want one or isn't capable of one can destroy your self-esteem and prevent you from living a healthy and productive life.

Staying Can Cause You Physical Harm

Staying in a destructive relationship causes continual stress and can be physically harmful. Unrelieved stress leaves us feeling "tied up in knots." We're on alert with high anxiety on a regular basis. Unrelieved stress causes some people to feel tired much of the time. You may also get frequent headaches, backaches, and stomachaches. You might worry frequently; eat too much, or not enough. Some people break out in rashes not related to allergies. Others cry or get angry a lot. Still others develop drug and alcohol dependency. Although leaving one of these relationships is a positive change, it's initially stressful and will take time to adjust to. Make sure you make your health a top priority and try to get at least eight hours of sleep at night along with regular moderate exercise. Also try to cut back on caffeine as it triggers the release of stress hormones.

Addicted to the Relationship?

Some people want out of destructive relationships but end up staying. On one hand they want out, on the other hand, there is a stronger pull to continue on as before. In other words, the relationship is addictive.

I knew for the last ten years of my nineteen year marriage I would be better off if I left. I knew it was an unhealthy relationship but was completely overwhelmed if I even entertained the idea of leaving. I thought I was imagining that life was miserable and that I wasn't trying hard enough. I felt leaving the marriage was admitting I was a failure as a wife and mother. It became a tug of war between what I thought I should do and what I knew deep down I had to do.

I also wasn't prepared emotionally or mentally to date once I left my marriage. I hadn't taken enough time to seriously consider what I wanted in a dating partner. I was more concerned with whether or not the person I dated was interested in dating me. I thought about things like fun, excitement, attractiveness. My approach to dating was naïve and reckless. If I saw an obvious red flag there was a tendency to dismiss it opting instead to give dating partners the benefit of the doubt even when it was clear I shouldn't.

There are signs of addiction in a relationship:

1. You know the relationship is bad for you but don't take effective steps to end it.
2. You make excuses for staying in the relationship that are weak or not accurate and not enough to counteract the harmful aspects.
3. You become anxious and fearful when you think about ending the relationship.
4. When you take steps to end the relationship, you suffer withdrawal which includes physical discomfort only relieved by reestablishing contact.

Another reason people stay in bad relationships is because much of their identity comes from being in the partnership. Without the relationship they face the daunting task of developing a new identity. They may also feel they have failed if they leave:

For me it was a belief I was a failure if I didn't stay. I believed I had to stay to prove I was a valuable person. My self-worth and identity hinged on being in a relationship and any relationship was better than none. I didn't see new possibilities.

Consequently, I had great fear of facing life without a partner. I didn't believe it was possible to put together a great life for myself.

Another reason people stay is because they get stuck. Feelings of being stuck don't happen because we get into to bad relationships as adults. Stuck feelings happen because they have been with us since childhood. Children do well when they are loved, nurtured, and encouraged to be independent. If parents are successful in doing this children will feel secure moving in and out of relationships. If these needs aren't met children may be needy and vulnerable to dependent relationships as adults.

When you're unhappy in your significant relationship all other parts of your life are affected. You won't live a healthy life if you're unhappy. Stress wears people out. Destructive relationships are exhausting and will not improve without effort from both people. If you have repeatedly attempted to leave a relationship and can't break free, realize your circumstances won't get better without taking action. Consider counseling. If you have a pattern of jumping from one bad relationship to another you may also need ongoing counseling to break it.

Find Outlets for Your Caring Nature

Most people would agree that caring about and for

others is an attribute to strive for. Parents want to raise caring children. We want our children to be interested in the community and world they live in. However, there are limits to how kind any person should be. At some point even the most caring individual has to say, enough is enough! No one wants to give and give getting very little or nothing in return. There has to be balance.

People who get into relationships with abusers tend to be optimistic to a fault. They believe no matter how bad their relationship is it will get better. Their partner will become kinder, gentler, more compromising and will suddenly "see the light." They have Pollyanna thinking and believe the person they care for will wake up one morning and decide to change their ways and do whatever it takes to have a healthy relationship. However, *there is a high probability this won't happen.* Abusers seek partners they can control. They can't sustain a positive relationship where conflict is managed effectively and mutual love and respect is the norm.

If you are committed to staying away from the relationship and want outlets for your caring nature, the next section will help with this. However, remember to care for yourself first. Take steps to get healthy and maintain that health.

Ten Causes I Care About

This list can be about anything. There is most likely a group out there that cares about whatever you may be interested in. Do you care about global warming? How about wastewater management? Do you have an interest in the concerns of children, animals, or the environment? Are there illnesses that afflict the elderly or cancer research you would like to know more about? I recently read an article in the local paper about a man who loved trees. He is known as the tree guy because he is passionate about trees. He has saved many from being cut down.

Take a moment to think of ten causes you care about:

1. 6.
2. 7.
3. 8.
4. 9.
5. 10.

Out of this list circle three to five causes that jump out at you and that you would be willing to investigate further. In an internet search see if you can find a local agency or organization and get the contact information. If you are interested, find out what opportunities are available to you. How much time are you willing to give? If there is a local group, attend several meetings. Three meetings will probably be enough to determine if this is something you want to pursue.

If you discover you're not as interested as you thought you were, try one of the other causes you circled. The point is to find something that interests you and that you're willing to give your time and effort to.

Don't Forget to Care about Yourself First

Again, some people are so focused on caring for others they don't take time to care for themselves. They learn early in life that caring about and for others is desirable. They sacrifice their own well being by placing too much value on helping others. People will learn to value you about as much as you value yourself. You may have a relationship with a parent or spouse who you are forever trying to please. It is better to please yourself first. It isn't selfish to take care of you:

I had a difficult time leaving the last relationship. There were times when he would do something thoughtful and I would decide he was showing he still cared. Other times I didn't see him for days and weeks at a time or there were behaviors that should have signaled to me that I needed to pay attention.

One time in particular sticks out for me as a turning

point. I had a bad cold and asked him to bring me cold medication. I was hoping he would bring it then stay for awhile. He brought it over but only stayed a minute. He was in a hurry because he had made other plans. That's when it hit me: I had been accepting the relationship on his terms, and what he wanted wasn't at all what I wanted. This wasn't about him being the bad guy and me being the victim; it was about my refusal to face reality. The reality was that I wanted a relationship partner; what I had was an activity partner. I was resentful of him being who he had been all along. It took me way too long to face the truth, and as a result, stayed in a bad situation much longer than I should have.

I wasn't taking care of myself. I was telling him over and over through my actions and words that the relationship was fine the way it was. I should have stated what I needed and wanted at the beginning.

Taking care of yourself will sometimes mean saying no to someone who wants to date you. It will sometimes mean ending a relationship you realize isn't right for you. It is always best to recognize the relationship for what it is early on. Pay attention to your red flags and gut instincts. By doing so, you will know what you need to do sooner rather than later.

Chapter 9
Relapsing

Don't Beat Yourself Up about Making Contact

Some people who have left destructive relationships resume contact and even go back to the relationship. They had a huge emotional investment in the relationship and when it fails suffer a big loss. They may feel great frustration for initiating contact, and in some instances, resuming the relationship. Don't feel bad about making the contact or resuming the partnership. Leaving usually involves a series of steps with each earlier step providing a foundation for subsequent progress. There are countless things we learn to do in life that take practice before we feel like we understand the process. Here is an example:

There are things in life we're expected to do but when it comes down to it have little preparation for. Going to a new job is one of them; it's not that easy. You think about going the day before since an alarm usually needs to be set. Then you wake up, get ready, and head out the door. Depending on what mode of transportation is used, getting to the job can be just as challenging as learning the actual job responsibilities. Next, there's the anxiety of meeting new people and hoping you'll fit in with the rest of the team.

Just learning to go to work is a process. It takes time. When I went back into the workforce I was eager, excited to learn, and anxious to prove I could be a quality employee. It was hard to be patient and accept that it would take time to develop an understanding of my new role, learn my responsibilities, and settle into the routine of going to work. Going to a new job is a big change whether we admit it or not and the transition isn't always smooth. It's an adjustment to have the job, adapt to it, and commit to going on a regular basis.

Adjusting to a new job is a process. Ending a relationship and committing to no contact is too. If you've maintained no contact then relapse and make contact again, you don't need to despair. It can take several or more attempts to leave a relationship for good. Maybe you need to take a look at what makes you vulnerable when it comes to reviving the contact. Are there supportive friends or family you can call if the urge is especially strong? Use your resources when you need to. Keep the focus on your life and your goals. Maybe you initiated contact but it doesn't matter, this is a process.

What Prompted the Call?

What happened that caused you to feel a strong urge to contact this person? Sometimes we become sentimental and our feelings take over.

Maybe he drove by your home or called and left a message. He may be ill or lost his job. He may have been evicted from his apartment or lost his house. A close relative may have become ill or died. Maybe he is roaming the streets, homeless. He could have told you anything. The fact is, now contact has resumed.

How Did the Call Go?

Chances are the call was friendly or at least civil. If he hasn't had contact with you in a while he probably misses you. He may also think you've had time to forget why you ended contact in the first place. How composed were you during the call? How long was the conversation? Were plans made for another conversation? Did you make plans to meet?

After the Call

After the phone call you are most likely thinking about him and his circumstances. It's likely he told you about some of the good going on in his life as well as his struggles. Right now get yourself back on track by switching gears. Get back to what you were doing before you made the call. Go back to Chapter 3 and read about staying in the moment. Look at the ideas listed for avoiding impulse contact. This gives you ideas of other things to do right now. Getting involved in another activity keeps you focused on what is going on in the here and now. The call is over. Treat it as if it were a call made to schedule a dentist appointment.

If You Made Plans to Meet

During the course of the conversation you may have made plans to meet. If so, decide if you'll follow through with your plans or cancel them. If you do want to meet I suggest making it brief to let him know you're moving forward with your life. If you're having second thoughts about meeting that is most likely enough of a red flag to signal it's best to cancel your plans. When you make the call to cancel simply state you've decided not to meet and end the call.

It Was Great for a While; Now I'm Back Where I Started

As was stated previously, it is a process to leave a long term relationship. You've invested your time, effort, and emotion into this person. Leaving is a life altering event and most likely a decision you have spent days, weeks, months, or years thinking about.

It won't do any good to get upset for having made contact. To take it a step further, you may have decided to resume the relationship. If this person has convinced you they want to make an effort to work on themselves and are willing to commit to at least six months of individual counseling there may be a foundation to build on. If, on the other hand, they start out with good intentions but then stop the counseling, it was most likely a smokescreen and they aren't likely to continue the therapy.

Panicking

Sometimes we go back to bad relationships and try one more time because we're anxious. In fact, we're so anxious to make a connection with someone, anyone, we are willing to go back to something familiar even if it was unhealthy. We believe life is about connecting, and if we don't happen to be connecting at the moment, it's reason enough to get back into an abusive relationship.

Based on my personal experiences I believe it's better to take time getting reacquainted with you and connecting with others who over time have proven to be on your side. Connect with people who genuinely care about you; they won't leave you hanging. Continue to focus on your healing and stay on an even keel. You may not have a partner in your life right now; you may not have one in six months, a year, or longer. However, the time you take to invest in yourself and your future, will bring rewards down the road. Also do your best to work toward taking care of yourself financially. For many years I didn't think I would be able to support myself. I was afraid, lacked confidence in my abilities, believed it was too difficult, and that I couldn't do it. As a result, I spent many years leaning on a man who saw me as a financial liability.

It is risky to lean on another person financially. At some point most anyone who depends on another person for financial support will be responsible for supporting themselves. A large number of older women depend on social security and retirement pensions as a means of support during their later years. Overall, older women have dramatically lower incomes than older men largely because they have had a lifelong pattern of economic dependency on men. Women of any age, but especially those over the age of forty, would be wise to secure their own financial futures before entering a new relationship. As a woman ages she will find men who are attracted to neediness and will more or less accommodate her desire to be taken care of. The price she pays for that care, however, could be high: emotional and mental abuse, physical abuse, or coerced sex. It's just not worth it.

When making connections with others search for a person who will connect with you in a loving way. Don't go into your search out of panic about not having a partner or because of financial difficulties. Be comfortable in your own skin. Develop a life you're proud of and is of your own choosing. Finding and having love from another human being is what we all want; just make sure you are content with where you are in life before joining forces with someone else.

Chapter 10

Getting Back on the Horse

Moving Forward Again

If you have decided you're ready to move forward and leave this person behind there will again be a period of adjustment. Spend as little time as possible thinking about this person. You'll most likely have thoughts about what went wrong or what you could have done to change the outcome; however, limit the time you spend rehashing the circumstances.

If after two months, you feel as miserable as you did after the first week you left, or your mood is affecting your work or making it difficult to take care of yourself and/or your family, you may be suffering from clinical depression. If that's the case, consider consulting a psychologist, psychiatrist, or family therapist.

Reread Chapter 5, Processing the Loss & Making Changes and Chapter 6, You're Unique! You've grown a lot and need to remind yourself often.

More Resolve with No Contact

Maybe you're at the point where it takes little effort at all to maintain no contact with your ex- partner. You've moved forward. If there are no children involved or you don't see your ex-partner in a work related setting, moving forward is easier. You may still have moments when you think about memories involving your past partner but these memories don't stir up the intense feelings they once did. You have come a long way!

Relax

After leaving the last relationship I felt the need to spend some extra time alone. It paid off as I learned to enjoy the solitude. I read, journaled, and worked on projects. I took myself out when I felt like it and in general took more time for my own needs

If you feel uncomfortable by yourself that may signal it's just the thing you need. You have so much information to process and if you have spent years raising children and bound to an unhealthy partnership you most likely haven't been spending much time in your own company. I felt anxious much of the time in my last two relationships as in both cases the relationships were highly activity based. It was difficult to spend time just hanging out and relaxing. Sure sometimes I enjoyed all the activity but I also needed down time without guilt as well.

If you've had little opportunity to relax take the time to do it now. Do things you love doing or nothing at all. Allow yourself time where you don't feel pressure to do anything. If you feel relaxed and love every minute it's a good indicator you're right on target.

Finding Joy

We don't need to be securely settled into a partnership to find joy in our lives. We can find it by ourselves. This isn't a cheap imitation of joy, it is the real thing!

One weekend I decided to go on a bike ride with an organized group of cyclists. The ride was on the back roads of Oregon vineyard country. I took the shortest ride, 35 miles. It was a hot day for a bike ride but there were rest stops a long the way and I took my time.

The ride was nice but even better was coming home knowing I could sink into my couch and relax next to my dog with no other care in the world.

It's a gift to live those moments because we realize we can create our own joy.

Pursue Your Own Adventures

In Chapter 6 you looked at your unique qualities and at current or new interests. Did you discover an interest you would like to explore further?

Have you ever thought: "I don't know what to do with myself?" Sometimes it is difficult to figure out what to do with our time. A million ideas go around in our minds and just when we think we've settled on one, we think of a reason why it won't work.

It is possible we get stuck in bad relationships because we want something interesting and exciting to do. We meet someone who seems almost manic in their ability to create new adventure. We buy into it and let go of our own interests or put them on the back burner in order to become involved in someone else's pursuits. There is nothing wrong with learning about and becoming involved in a new partner's interests as long as we continue to pursue the things we've always enjoyed. The things we do on our own are just as thrilling and exciting as the things we do with others. It's all a matter of our perception.

Being Different

Breaking any pattern takes effort. It's natural to pick what we're familiar with. We'll continue to be attracted to the same types of people until we choose to change our selection process. Practice doing something different every day. If you normally get up on the right side of the bed, get up on the left. If you usually take a shower, take a bath once in awhile. If you have corn flakes for breakfast, eat any kind of cereal but that one. If you like to read your email before going to work, try reading it when you get home. The objective is to change your patterns.

My youngest son used to love to eat out at the same restaurant 100 percent of the time. He said he loved it there and didn't see a reason to try another one. I liked it too but not every time! It took awhile for him to feel comfortable going to other restaurants.

It can go like this with relationship partners. We don't intentionally set ourselves up for a bad experience, it's more that we get into a pattern and don't recognize it right away. It's natural to go with what is familiar to us. We feel comfortable with what we're used to and most likely gravitate toward the same type of partner on a subconscious level.

Practice change in all aspects of your life. Try something different: a different dessert; a different route to work; rearrange your living room; try going to a different grocery store. Start small and progress. Keep a calendar and document all of the changes you make. Be proud of all the small changes you are making and remember that change is about taking small steps. Change takes time, sometimes years, and the bigger the change the longer it takes. When you were one and learning to walk you took a couple of steps fell down and then got up again. It's the same way now. The changes you make will come in due time if you are serious about making them. If you find you've made a change and don't like it, try something else. Forget perfection. You'll learn while you make mistakes and will gradually become conditioned to the changes.

Chapter 11

In a Hurry for Love?

Know Who You Are

Knowing yourself well takes time. Make sure you feel fine in your own company before searching for a new relationship partner. The best love connections are between two independent individuals bringing out the best in each other. There's no need to cling to a new person. If you attach yourself too early to a man you barely know, you will most likely drive him away or realize shortly afterward that you may have a new partner, but the same issues keep cropping up for you. Take some time to examine your head and your heart. If you understand where you are coming from you will be more careful when meeting new people and deliberate longer before entering into a new relationship. Some people feel they can change a new partner. They believe that given enough time and effort they can mold their partner to be who they want them to be. This isn't likely to happen but some people believe their individual situation is different and believe they should force changes to make a new partner more to their liking. The result may be an ongoing tug of war. Small changes can and do happen over time. Going into a new relationship and discovering you have little common ground with a new person is disappointing but it is better to face it than frustrate them and yourself by trying to force quick change. See yourself and the new person in a realistic light.

Addicted to Love

In Chapter 8 relationship addiction was discussed. Another addiction is one to love. The word cathexis is used to describe the concentration of emotional energy onto an object or idea. This word has also been used to describe the powerful emotional experience known as "falling in love." Suddenly everything is beautiful and we are one with the universe. Nothing has really changed but our perception. We may barely know this new person we have fallen for but love the way we feel when we're with them. We may go to great lengths to keep the relationship going. It becomes like a drug. We may change our behavior or the way we dress. We may feign interest in new hobbies or pastimes in order to be more appealing to them.

Once the relationship is established we'll struggle to hide anything that appears to be out of whack. Friends may tease and comment about new interests even though we tell them we've always been like this. An example would be an ordinarily quiet studious woman who loves wearing comfortable sweaters, reading, and going to bookstore lectures, meets a Hell's Angels type. She swaps the sweaters and books for a leather jacket and a Harley.

Robin Norwood, in her excellent book <u>Women Who Love Too Much</u> outlines a ten step plan for overcoming love addiction. The first of these ten steps is:

Make your recovery your first priority in your life

Please refer to her book for the remaining nine steps.

The best choices for partners are people who are most like us. If we don't have to alter our likes and dislikes to suit the whims of a new partner we're closer to being on track than if we alter our natural self to meet the expectations of someone new.

The Attraction Factor

Attraction seems to be an accumulation of different things. Physical attraction is necessary to get interested in the first place; however, we should have specific qualities in mind when searching for a partner. What is important to us? Of course we want someone who has interests similar to our own. When searching for a relationship partner you will meet a variety of men each with their own unique style. Some will likely be fun to go out with but not a wise partner choice. The more experienced you become meeting and communicating with different types of men the more attuned you become to people in general. You may come out of a difficult relationship viewing all men as exactly like the one you left. You may lack trust in your ability to know which men are healthy for you. By getting to know you and gaining trust and confidence in your ability to judge character, the better able you will be to choose a partner who will be a good fit for you.

Online dating websites are an option. The more time you spend communicating the more relaxed you will be chatting with or emailing new people. At first it may seem awkward and unnatural but it is all part of making change. Experiment with different conversation starters. Shy away from predictability and ask questions. The objective isn't to alter who you are, but to think differently and gain a new perspective about meeting, selecting, and dating.

No Contact

You want a person that is right for you and by communicating with a variety of people you will learn which personality styles suit you best. Be cautious with men who talk a lot about physical attractiveness: their own and what they want in a woman. Sure, there has to be a level of physical attraction but there is more to a relationship than that. If a man focuses primarily on physical attractiveness he's most likely looking for a physical relationship only. Communicate with new men as you would any friend. Keep it light and fun. Find out about their interests and their outlook on life.

Learn to Say No

Saying no isn't easy in the dating world. In fact, some people say yes when they really mean no because they worry about tactfully rejecting someone. Others say maybe, knowing that when it gets right down to it no is what they mean, but want to keep the possibility open. It is vital to your future happiness to learn how to say no so you will meet people you want to say yes to. If you stay in relationships with people you know are not right for you, you miss out on a great relationship with someone who is.

On the other hand, sometimes we disconnect from new people too early because we don't feel immediately attracted to them. Consequently, we don't get to know things about them that could make us do an about face.

If you have given a new person a fair chance, say four dates, there are no shared interests, and you feel little or no attraction, you will most likely want to move on.

Remember to pay attention to your instincts and don't be taken in by charm. Narcissists are very adept at taking on chameleon characteristics. Initially, they adjust their likes and dislikes in order to accommodate you. Also be cautious around people who want to monopolize your time. If they want to spend every spare moment with you it should be a huge red flag. No one should initially want to eat up all your free time. Tell them no. Let them know up front you want to spend quality time with them but not all of your time. The key is balance. If they refuse to accept that boundary, get out.

Again, give people whom you don't initially feel attracted to a chance. Get to know them even though you don't feel sparks right off the bat. Getting to know another person in various settings helps you relate to them and as you relate, you can become attracted. There is a lot to be said for getting to know a man who likes to have fun in the same ways you do and makes jokes you find funny. Maybe you like night life; maybe you like to mountain bike. If he likes to enjoy himself in the same ways you do there is potential.

If you do decide to say no to someone do so tactfully but firmly. Be as straightforward as possible. They will initially be disappointed but will respect your ability to be honest.

Zero Tolerance for Abuse

When dating it should be standard practice that any new person brings their best self forward on the first date. However, on the second, third, and fourth dates it's likely that some of their more undesirable qualities begin to surface. Maybe he apologizes because he forgot his wallet, tells you he'll pay you back, and asks you to foot the bill. Is he critical of your appearance? Does he suggest you would look better in another style of clothing? Asks if you've thought of wearing your hair up or down, growing it long, or cutting it short. Does he get irate in slow traffic? There could be a gentle or not so gentle shove. One isolated incident doesn't necessarily mean this person is abusive but if you hear unsettling comments or his actions give you cause for concern, take heed.

Also pay attention to how at ease you feel when you're with him. Are you relaxed or do you often feel some tension? Do they want to touch you/show affection right off the bat? Let them know up front you're not interested in any physical contact while you get to know them.

How do they react to that boundary? If they seem irritated or put off you may want to steer clear.

Are you able to ask him questions? Some people feel it's not polite to ask questions so hesitate. They feel it's too aggressive but without questions it will be nearly impossible to get to know a new person. You won't get to know anyone if you don't ask them about their likes and dislikes. However, prying by either person should be avoided. It isn't necessary to ask any new person about previous relationships. Asking questions about their interests, work, hobbies, pets, childhood dreams, however, is a good idea. How a person responds to your questions is a good indicator of how they view questions in general and how interested they are in you. A person who is irritated by question and answer conversation may have something to hide or is uncomfortable giving and receiving information or just isn't interested in pursuing a relationship with you. A new person should be glad you're making the effort to get to know them better.

Stating Opinions

As when coming out of a destructive relationship, it can also be difficult in a new dating relationship to say what we think. It's tough to stand by an opinion which is different from that of a new person. Don't be afraid to say what you think. I once met a man who was a serious motorcycle rider. He told me he didn't ride much in the winter but spent a lot of time riding during the summer months. He asked me my opinion of motorcycles. At the time I remember thinking, I could tell him I loved them and perhaps have further contact but instead said it depends on the rider and that motorcycle safety is a big issue with me.

I didn't have further contact with him. He may have believed I wasn't someone he wanted to get to know because I wasn't enthusiastic about motorcycles.

Be honest with people and tell them what you think. It isn't always pleasant but it doesn't have to be awkward either. You are gaining confidence and letting people know who you are. It's a smart thing to do. You won't have the same interests as every man you meet. Your intent is to select people who are compatible with you. Not to be an everywoman for everyman.

You've Met Someone New

You have been meeting new people and have met someone you feel you would like to get to know better. Great! You've taken a big step and are moving onto new relationships. You will want to spend some quality time with him but take it slow. You have a lot to offer any new person and don't need to hurry the process along. Continue doing the things in your own life you love doing. This person should enhance your life, not cause additional stress or make you feel guilty for continuing with your interests and hobbies. He will also be observing you and taking note of how involved you are in your own life. If you seem too eager to spend all your free time with him he might assume you had no life before he came along.

How Do You Feel?

Pay attention to how you feel with a new person. Does he respect you, your friends, and family? How does he interact when you introduce him to the other people in your life? Do you feel relaxed in his presence? Do you look forward to your time with him?

Do you make excuses for him and his behavior? Look over the list of red flags in Chapter 5. Make sure he is someone you genuinely feel good about. Do you have an underlying feeling of being uncomfortable that doesn't go away? Does he have follow through: does he do what he says he's going to do, not just with you but with other people in his life? If red flags come up for you discuss them with him. If you don't feel comfortable enough to discuss the red flags that may be the biggest red flag of all!

No Contact

Early Red Flags

- Monopolizes conversations
- Insults others in your presence
- Insults you, your appearance
- Regularly gives unsolicited advice
- Abuses alcohol and drugs
- Might have come from an abusive family
- Abused previous partners
- Cruel to children and animals
- Wants quick involvement
- Is extremely possessive and jealous
- Controlling
- Has mood swings
- Has a short temper
- Easily angered
- Low self-esteem
- Makes accusations of cheating or dishonesty
- Poor listener
- Selective memory – doesn't recall events accurately or insists certain events never took place
- Isolates from others
- Makes most if not all decisions
- Checks up on other person constantly – may follow and watch other person
- Attempts to control partner's contact with other people
- Blames others for his/her problems
- Believes in rigid sex roles (men dominant, women submissive)

- Excessive ranting
- Quick to judge decisions you make early in the relationship

Teens experiencing dating violence may:

- Have failing grades
- Begin skipping classes or drop out of school
- Show changes in personality or in mood
- Begin using drugs/alcohol
- Begin isolating from friends and family
- Emotional outbursts

Remember to meet new people in a public place, never in yours or their home. Your safety is always top priority! Because you have previously been involved in a difficult/abusive relationship, you will most likely be familiar with some of the above warning signs and may have more. Pay attention to all these indicators.

Avoid Becoming Sidetracked

New relationships are exciting as you get to know a new person. You learn a lot about them including what they like to do in regard to their interests and hobbies. It's also a good time for them to get to know about you and what you enjoy doing as your interests are equally important. Whatever you were doing before you met this person is what you should continue to do. Do they encourage you to give up previous interests and activities? Neither of you should have to pretend to like something you don't, give up spending time with your friends, or drop out of activities you enjoy. You should also feel free to develop new talents interests and friends. In general, you should be able to move forward with your life.

In one previous relationship I continued to go to church during the first year. The second year it became a struggle and I let it slide. I made the choice to participate in activities with my partner on Sunday mornings. It didn't matter that he usually planned these activities what mattered is that I went along with it. It was my responsibility to stick with my boundary and I didn't. Initially, I continued going. Over time, my church attendance became less regular until eventually I stopped going altogether. I wasn't firm in my decision to continue with an activity I had previously loved. I had weak boundaries. I gave it up because I believed it was more important to spend Sunday mornings with my partner.

Staying intact after entering a new relationship is important. It's a good idea to mentally schedule routine check-ins to make sure you're making decisions you want to make and if not, why? Things do change over time and you may find you're not as interested in an activity you previously enjoyed. But ask yourself if you would still give up an activity if you're partner weren't in your life. Make sure you can honestly say you're living life on your own terms by participating in activities you enjoy, and maintaining interests you love, regardless of whether or not your partner participates.

Appearances Can Be Deceiving

Reading online dating website profiles is a great way to figure out which types of people appeal to you. What do they mention in terms of their interests? What do you mention in terms of your interests? Lots of dating profiles contain many of the same interest words such as music, movies, friends, family, outdoors, reading etc. Some profiles are enjoyable to read and seem genuine. Other profiles steer us away. There are profiles in which both men and women focus on what they don't like and don't want instead of what they enjoy doing and traits they're looking for in a partner. It can make the reader feel defensive right off the bat.

Still other profiles are disarming. Depending on the wording, I sometimes cringe when I read a profile where the man says, "I know how to treat a lady." When reading this I assume the man believes most men don't know how to treat a lady and are not true gentlemen.

No Contact

In some social structures years ago, men would attempt during courtship, to win the affections of women who came from families of influence, power, and money. They would try to outdo other suitors with gentlemanly ways. In turn the new bride would bring money and property to her husband in marriage.

Today it seems that some men still bring the courtship behaviors, though courtship isn't always part of the plan. These men may believe women want them to appear to be gentlemen. However, it would seem that women would rather date men who are nice to be with, value them, and are considerate of their feelings. Some men have appeared to be gentlemen as a way to meet and sleep with as many women as possible. They may want to "show up well" even though there is no actual courtship intended. The woman often plays a role in this because she goes along with it.

All and all, a kind and caring person has a deeper relationship with those in his or her life. Showing up in brand name clothing, using gestures like flowers and wine, opening car doors, and other pleasantries are nice, but there should be more. Chivalry isn't really relationship building material. Look for the person who doesn't spend a whole lot of time on pretense. You can be yourself and show emotion; you're able to laugh or cry in their presence. Seek a person who doesn't vacillate between extreme highs and lows and instead shows consistency in their personality. You should be able to count on them to do what they say they will and are not in need of constant activity and excitement.

In the news some time back, there was a story about a man who was a member of a popular dating website, posing as a physician. He even went to the trouble of dressing the part while visiting one of the women he was dating in a hospital, where she was a patient. As it turned out, he wasn't a physician, but a rapist, who drugged women he dated, then raped them. These women believed what he told them. He was good looking, wore nice clothes, and was convincing in presenting himself to be all that he said he was.

Those of us who have been in relationships with narcissists know they use pretense. Their use of romance and gentlemanly appearances are very effective in winning over new partners. In the beginning, a narcissist may appear to be the nicest guy you could ever meet and treat you like a queen. However, it doesn't take long for the other guy—the manipulative, mean tempered, devaluing, out of control one, to make an appearance. Narcissists have a Jekyll and Hyde nature. It is easy to believe that the nice guy is the real or the true self but the reality is that the nice guy and the bad guy are both part of the false self. The narcissist doesn't have a real self. He is empty. He doesn't have a clue about who he is and couldn't care less. They do not have the desire to make another person happy. They are all about appearances and must also have power over others. They don't care if you love, fear, or hate them. What is important to them is that they have control.

Background Checks

Do your own research on any new person you meet. Get as much information as possible. You can do this by typing their name into a search engine or by contacting your state or local government agencies to get public information. You can also use paid services found online or through local yellow pages to obtain a full background report. When using one of these services do your homework. Make sure you are paying for a service that produces accurate results. Use good judgment when communicating with men on dating websites. There is one dating site known for doing criminal and marriage checks: a warning on True.com reads: "We can't guarantee criminals won't get on the site, but we can guarantee they'll be sorry if they do."

Meet any new person in a public place preferably during the day. Probably one hour is a reasonable amount of time for a first meeting.

Use common sense. Pay attention to details someone shares with you and if you find anything that doesn't add up ask questions. If your questions are ignored or they are evasive or you question their responses to your questions, end the contact.

Balance in the Relationship

All relationships need balance. In your significant relationship with a partner, this balance will determine whether your relationship is successful.
Observe yourself in the partnership. How much emotional space do you take up? Is one person more involved than the other? Is one expressing more emotion than the other? If one person is intense and needy while the other is uninvolved, the relationship is out of whack. The emotional life of the relationship needs to be generated by two people as equally as possible; otherwise it is lopsided with both people unhappy. One is working too hard and the other feels like they can't get a break from the intensity.

If you are working too hard you prevent your partner from participating; step back. Take some time to meet your needs with others outside the relationship. Talk to friends or family or write in a journal. Ask for some of your needs to be met inside the relationship but not all of them. Shift some of your emotional needs to others.

Watch for too much intensity by you *and* your partner. It can be exhausting over the long haul if both people generate too much drama on a regular basis.

No Contact

Both of you will need to tone down the emotions, needs, wants, upsets.

On the other hand, if neither person takes up any emotional space, or reaches a particular level and stays there, the relationship may be okay but there isn't any real depth. In this case, it might be best to start out small and share something that you haven't shared up to now. See if your partner follows your lead. If not, decide if this is the right relationship for you.

Chapter 12
Testing 1, 2, 3...

Remember to Live Your Life

I have heard people talk about all the things they will do once they have someone special in their lives. Don't wait! Do them now! Every day of our lives we are growing, not just when we are children. Continue your education. Learn a language. Take dance lessons or learn to paint draw or play an instrument. Write a novel. Remodel your house. There are many possibilities. Think about your interests. Keep yourself growing!

Putting your life on hold while waiting for a special person to come along keeps you dependent on others. You're completely capable of creating an excellent life. If you wait for someone else to make your life better instead of plunging forward and making it better for yourself, depression and loneliness will follow. You have everything you need to have a great life. Take advantage of all the strength you have gained as part of this process. Remember to stay grounded, take care of yourself, give to others, and have goals. Enjoy what you are doing in your own life. Your passions and interests are what set you apart from everyone else in the world. Make it a priority to focus on you and give yourself time to do what you want on a regular basis.

Use Your Head!

Remember from the previous chapter that balance is the key to successful relationships. Balance your heart and head when it comes to new relationships. Pay attention to what you think and how you feel about a new person. By now, you have ended contact with a former relationship partner and have spent time reflecting, healing, and making changes. You have a better understanding of what you want and are gaining a new appreciation and acceptance of yourself. You have also thought about your interests and how you enjoy spending your time. Keep the evaluation process going but don't forget to get out there, enjoy friendships, and have fun.

Physical Intimacy in a New Relationship

Refrain from physical intimacy in a new relationship as it shouldn't be part of getting to know a new person. If anything it makes getting to know them almost impossible. You want to feel comfortable and relaxed with someone new. Are there mutual likes and dislikes? Is there mutual giving and sharing? Do you view this person as a friend? Do you enjoy spending time with them?

Are they easy to talk to? Is there anything about them that makes you feel uncomfortable? Take time to really get to know any new person. When you take more time to bond you protect yourself from getting attached too soon.

Communication

Meeting a new person should be exciting and fun although it can also bring on some feelings of nervousness or apprehension. Will they find you attractive? Will you make a lasting impression with your personality? Too much concern about how you appear to the other person is not where you want your focus. Focus on getting to know them. You have a great opportunity to observe and in turn learn about them. They may wear a particular style of clothing which is unique to them; they may have a great smile, and/or voice. Notice qualities in new people because it sets you apart and makes the other person feel special. There are plenty of great people in the world. Developing the skill of noticing others gives you an advantage. It also allows you to assert your personality. If the other person doesn't respond to you in a way you would like, don't let it rattle you. Maintain your poise. Remember, not all people you go out with will be right for you. Your ability to live in the moment will be of benefit with each new person you meet. Be true to yourself by being yourself as best you can around new people.

Rejection

Many of us stay in destructive relationships because we fear being alone. We also fear moving forward and facing possible rejection by new people. Being rejected is not a unique phenomenon but rather a part of life. We can't get to where we are supposed to be unless we learn to deal with and face rejection along the way. For some, rejection is debilitating. Learning to deal with setbacks and failure helps us become resilient. Building resiliency teaches us how to bounce back after having failed. Taking risks with relationships or in other areas of life is never a sure thing but you will live a fuller and richer life through your experiences. No rejection is easy and it's not welcome in dating even though it is better to learn early on that a new friendship won't develop further. By facing rejection and moving forward quickly you will be ready for the next opportunity that comes your way.

In today's dating world we can communicate on the internet with people we would not meet otherwise by building a rapport via chat or email. Sometimes great relationships develop this way. Other times, the initial meeting ends with no further communication online or in person.

It can be discouraging to be rejected by one or more dating partners. Sometimes we vow to give up meeting new people…

I remember meeting a man in person who I found through a newspaper dating site ad. He pushed for meeting after we had spoken on the phone just a couple of times and I went along with it. As soon as we sat down in the restaurant I wished I were somewhere else. He seemed quite bored with our conversation which was amazing considering he was barely participating. I learned quite a bit after that hour meeting. I learned that if I don't feel ready to meet a man, don't meet him until I am. I also learned that if the other person isn't interested enough to ask even one question or to make the slightest effort toward small talk, there is no reason for me to carry the conversation just to avoid the silence.

I didn't hear from this man again. This was actually the first man I met six months after my divorce. I was nervous before meeting him and am sure my nervousness was evident. It's best not to read anything into the rejection from one person or even a few. On the other hand, if you meet many men and are rejected by all of them, begin looking at the possibility that you're sending out vibes of low self-esteem. Remember what a great person you are and let it shine through. Relax and enjoy each opportunity as a great learning experience. Concentrate on learning about new people and whether you want to get to know them further. Again, concentrating on your appearance, and whether they think you're attractive, isn't where your focus should be. Put effort into looking your best before you meet then go and have fun. If it turns out to be disappointing, let it go. Give yourself credit for stepping up and taking a chance.

When You Reject

If you reject the other person do it respectfully but do it quickly. There is no reason to prolong a dating relationship if you know early on you're not interested. Too many women have stayed in relationships they wanted to leave simply because they didn't know how to get out. For a variety of reasons they knew early on they wanted to end it. They may have believed there was potential for abuse or felt the relationship was inappropriate in some other way, yet stayed, only to regret it later. If you know you are not at all sure of, or comfortable with a new person, leave. Don't worry about regretting your decision. Have enough confidence in your ability to make judgments that will benefit you. Remember, your opinion counts. Develop trust in your ability to make good decisions.

Life Isn't Always Exciting but It Is a Precious Gift

Sometimes we get into inappropriate relationships because we start to feel like life just isn't as exciting as we think it should be. We may even dismiss a relationship with an appropriate person because they don't seem exciting enough for us. If you are looking for excitement find a hobby that is thrilling for you. Don't discount your own ability to make your life stimulating.

Every breath we take extends our time on earth. It's an amazing gift that we are here! If you're in reasonably good health, able to get out of bed in the morning, get dressed, and head out the door, be thankful for it. Be glad you're independent enough to leave your home and get to your destination. There are those who are not so fortunate. They may be gravely ill or disabled to the point where living what the rest of us would consider a "normal" life is not possible. Be grateful for your health, your family, and your friends. Remember how wonderful it is to be alive.

Look at the opportunities you have right now. Enjoy your life despite circumstances that are not ideal and relationships that didn't work out. No matter where you are at this moment or how things look you have an opportunity to create a better life.

Whether you search for a partner through online dating, newspaper ads, meeting through friends, club activities, sports teams, night life, travel groups, classes, church etc. have fun while you're doing it. People are attracted to those who look like they're enjoying themselves. Sometimes you will feel you truly love your life; other times feeling positive will take a lot of effort. Remember, *you,* are in charge of your life. You have eliminated or are on your way to eliminating a destructive relationship. This means you are also eliminating a major stressor.

No Contact

Take your time and find people you enjoy being with and who appreciate you. Spend less time with critical people and more time with those who love, respect, and encourage you. Look for those who will listen to you even when you complain and will help you learn from failure. Remember that you are unique. Believe in yourself!

Final Thoughts

Many people have written guides to leaving destructive relationships, healing, and living a better life. The main thing I add to the mix is insight from my personal experiences and growth along the way. Growing towards me has not been an easy process. It should be natural to be who you were designed to be. If like me, you haven't been sure how to fit into your own life, get to know yourself before attempting to develop a new partnership.

Choosing a relationship partner is one of the biggest challenges any of us ever face. Some people make wise partner choices early in adulthood. They know what they want and trust their instincts enough to form partnerships with people they believe will provide stability friendship and love. They also know that the quality of their significant relationships is a precursor to a happy life. Other people end up going through life wishing they had made a wiser life partner choice but for many reasons decide to stay with the partner they did choose. Others divorce or are left widowed. This book has been written for those who want to leave a marriage, long term partnership, or dating relationship for their health and safety. The objective is to end contact quickly and permanently, or in the case of co-parenting or co-worker situations, keeping contact to a minimum as it relates to the children or to the work environment.

You are as important as anyone else who will ever enter your life. If you forget that fact you will struggle making decisions and living life in a way that is best for you. Sacrificing who you are for the sake of another person isn't a healthy choice.

Celebrate who you are and feel proud of all you have learned and overcome. Be careful who you let into your life and who you decide to trust. If you meet someone you would like as a relationship partner pay attention as you get to know them and trust your instincts. You are moving toward a healthy way of life for yourself. As a result *you* will benefit as will all of those people in your life now and the ones yet to come.

Traits Associated with Narcissistic Personality Disorder

There is a wealth of information online regarding this disorder. A Google search will provide you with more than enough options to introduce you to traits associated with the disorder. Most of the traits discussed apply to all narcissists however that doesn't mean that all the traits will apply to the narcissists you know.

Resources for Getting Out of a Destructive Relationship

The following are resources to help you. They are not all inclusive however the resources listed should provide valuable information to you. Each state also provides county resources.

WomensLaw.org

This site provides easy-to-understand legal information and resources to women living with or escaping domestic violence. The site publishes state-specific legal information for domestic violence. They also provide help through email, directly to women and advocates throughout the U.S.

National Domestic Violence Hotline
1-800-799-SAFE (7233)
1-800-787-3224 (TDD)

Domestic Violence 50 state Resource
www.dv911.com/dv50state.htm

www.womenshealth.gov
http://www.menstoppingviolence.org
The Stalking Victims' Sanctuary at
http://www.stalkingvictims.com

Women Helping Battered Women PO Box 1535, Burlington, VT 05402 Office 802-658-3131; Fax 802-658-3832; Hotline 802-658-1996 (TDD) www.whbw.org

http://www.aardvarc.org Abuse Rape and Domestic Violence Aid & Resource Collection. At this site you may enter your state into the search engine.

http://www.snow.org At the bottom of the page type in domestic violence information and then click on search.

State Resources

Alabama – The Alabama Coalition Against Domestic Violence 800-650-6522

Alabama – Alabama Coalition Against Domestic Rape 334-264-0123; 888-725-7273

Alabama – Child Support Services 334-242-9300 Volunteer Lawyers Program – 334-269-1515

Alaska – Alaska Network on Domestic Violence and Sexual Assault 800-799-7233

Alaska Office of Victim's Rights 866-2742620

No Contact

Alaska Family Law Self-Help Center 907-264-0851
Arizona Coalition Against Domestic Violence 800-782-6400
Arizona – Southern Arizona Center Against Sexual Assault 24-hour Sexual Assault Crisis Lines 520-327-7273 or 800-400-1001
Arkansas Coalition Against Domestic Violence 800-269-4668
Arkansas Access to Justice Commission 800-952-9243
Arkansas Legal Services Partnership 501-376-3423
California Alliance Against Domestic Violence 800-524-4765
Colorado Anti-Violence Program 303-839-5204
Colorado Coalition Against Domestic Violence (English/Espanola) 888-778-7091 or 303-831-9632
Colorado Coalition against Sexual Assault 303-861-7033
Colorado Organization for Victim Assistance 800-261-2682
Connecticut toll free domestic violence hotline 888-774-2900
Delaware Domestic Violence Advocacy Center Kent County 302-672-1075; Sussex County 302-856-5843 Support for court proceedings referrals and accompaniment to hearings
Delaware - Families in transition – Kent & Sussex Counties 302-422-8058 Emergency and transitional services, housing assistance, employment, transportation, educational services
District of Columbia City-wide Sexual Assault Hotline 202-333-RAPE

DC Crime Victims Compensation Program 202-879-4216

Florida – Domestic Violence Hotline – 800-500-1119

Florida – http://www.dcf.state.fl.us/domesticviolence/

Georgia – Emergency Shelter information call the 24 hour hotline 800-334-2836

Georgia – Battered Women's Justice Project 800-903-0111

Georgia – 4Sarah Resource Center 770-784-0708

Hawaii – State Coalition Against Domestic Violence Hilo – 808-959-8864; Kauai – 808-245-8404; Kona – 808-322-SAFE (322-7233); Wailuku 808-579-9581; Molokai 808-567-6888; Oahu 808-841-0822

Hawaii – www.hscadv.org

Idaho Council on Domestic Violence and Victim Assistance – 208-334-6512 toll-free 800-291-0463

Idaho Coalition Against Sexual & Domestic Violence; 300 E Mallard Dr. Ste. 130 Boise, Idaho 83706; 208-384-0419 toll free 888-293-6118

Illinois – Chicagoland Domestic Violence Help Line 877-863-6338

Illinois Coalition Against Domestic Violence 801 S. 11th St., Springfield, IL 62703; 217-789-2830

Indiana Coalition Against Domestic Violence 800-538-3393

Indiana Statewide Domestic Violence Hotline 800-332-7385

Iowa Coalition Against Domestic Violence 24-hour statewide hotline 800-942-0333

Kansas Coalition Against Sexual And Domestic Violence 785-232-9784

Kentucky Domestic Violence Association 502-209-5382

Louisiana Domestic Violence Hotline 888-411-1333

Maine – Statewide Domestic Violence Hotline 866-83-4HELP

Maine Coalition to End Domestic Violence; 170 Park Street, Bangor, ME 04401; Phone 207-941-1194; Fax 207-941-2327; Email: info@mcedv.org

Maine Coalition Against Sexual Assault; 83 Western Ave. Suite 2, Augusta, ME 04330; Phone 207-626-0034; Fax 207-626-5503

Maine Statewide Sexual Assault Hotline 800-871-7741 TTY 888-458-5599 Confidential 24 hour toll-free hotline accessible anywhere in Maine.

Maryland Network Against Domestic Violence; 6911 Laurel-Bowie Road Suite 309, Bowie, MD 20715 Phone 800-MD-HELPS or 301-352-4574 Fax 301-809-0422; Email info@mnadv.org

Maryland Crime Victims Resource Center 877-VICTIM-1

Maryland Family Violence Council Victim Services 410-821-2844

Massachusetts – Jane Doe, Inc – Massachusetts Coalition Against Domestic Violence; 14

Beacon Street, Suite 507, Boston, MA 02108 Toll-free phone #'s 800-223-5001 (Spanish) 800-688-4889 TTY in Spanish; 877-785-2020 (24 hr. hotline, toll-free in Massachusetts); email address: info@janedoe.org Web site address: http://www.janedoe.org/

Massachusetts Office of Victim Assistance – 1-617-727-5200

Michigan Coalition Against Domestic and Sexual Violence; 3893 Okemos Rd. Suite B2, Okemos, MI 48864; 517-347-7000 Fax 517-347-1377 TTY 517-381-8470

Michigan – The Listening Ear Crisis Hotline 517-337-1717 (24 hr Crisis Line)Michigan – Third Level Crisis Line 800-442-7315

Minnesota Coalition for Battered Women; 590 Park Street, Suite 410, St. Paul, MN 55103 Phone: 651-646-6177 or 800-289-6177.

Minnesota Crisis Connection; PO Box 19550, Minneapolis, MN 55419, Phone 612-379-6364; fax 612-379-6391 http://www.crisis.org

Minnesota Sexual Violence Center 24 hour crisis line 612-871-5111

Minnesota Chrysalis 4432 Chicago Ave S, Minneapolis, MN 55407 Phone 612-870-2420, fax 612-870-2403

http://www.chrysaliswomen.org Chrysalis is a multi-service organization serving women and their families.

Mississippi – S.A.F.E Inc. PO Box 985, Tupelo, MS 38802 662-841-9138

No Contact

Mississippi – Family Crisis Services of NWMS, Inc. PO Box 1698, Oxford, MS 38655

Mississippi- Our House, Inc. PO Box 3956, Greenville, MS 38704, Crisis line 662-332-5683 or 888-884-5683

Mississippi -Safe Haven, Inc. PO Box 5354, Columbus, MS 39704 662-327-2259

Mississippi – Catholic Charities, Inc. Rape Crisis Center, 200 North Congress Street, Suite 100, Jackson, MS 39201 Phone 601-948-4495; Crisis Line 601-982-7273

Mississippi – Wesley House Community Center, Inc. PO Box 1207, Meridian, MS 39302 601-485-2828 or 800-643-6250

Mississippi – The Guardian Sexual Assault Crisis Center, 126 S. Commerce St., Suite 103, Natchez, MS 39121 Phone 601-446-8668; Crisis Line 888-721-5460

Mississippi – The Shafer Center for Crisis Intervention, USM Box 10016, Hattiesburg, MS 39406 Phone 601-264-7078.

Mississippi – Gulf Coast Women's Center for Non-Violence PO Box 333, Biloxi, MS 39533, 228-436-3809

Missouri Coalition Against Domestic Violence, 415 E. McCarty Street, Jefferson City, MO 65101 Phone: 573-634-4161 FAX: 573-636-3728

Missouri – LEAD Institute (interpreter services for hearing-impaired domestic violence victims), 311 Bernadette Dr. Suite C, Columbia, MO 65203 Phone 573-445-5005 or 800-380-3323

Missouri – Elder Abuse Hotline, 3418 Knipp Dr. Jefferson City, MO 65109, Phone 800-392-0210

Missouri Coalition Against Sexual Assault, PO Box 104866, Jefferson City, MO 65110, Phone 877-7MoCASA

Montana Coalition Against Domestic and Sexual Violence PO Box 818, Helena, MT 59624 Phone: 406-443-7794 or 888-404-7794

Nebraska Domestic Violence Sexual Assault Coalition 825 M St, Suite 404, Lincoln, NE 68508 Phone 402-476-6256 help@ndvsac.org Call the following number to reach the domestic violence/sexual assault program serving your area 800-876-6238 Call 877-215-0167 for information in Spanish.

Nevada Domestic Violence Hotline 800-500-1556

Nevada Network Against Domestic Violence Se Habla Espanol 220 S. Rock Blvd, Suite 7, Reno, NV 89502 775-828-1115

Nevada Coalition Against Sexual Violence 741 Veterans Memorial Drive, Las Vegas, NV 89101 702-384-1005

New Hampshire Coalition Against Domestic & Sexual Violence 800-852-3388; 800-735-2964 – TDD/Voice

New Hampshire – Women's Information Service (WISE) 866-348-WISE (toll-free crisis line)

New Jersey Coalition for Battered Women 800-572-SAFE (7233)

New Jersey Battered Lesbian Hotline (NJ only) 800-224-0211.

New Jersey Office of Victim – Witness Advocacy 609-896-8855

New Mexico Coalition Against Domestic Violence 800-773-3645

New Mexico Dept. of Corrections Victim Services 877-842-8464

New Mexico Legal FACS 24 Hours Advocacy 505-217-0464

New Mexico Morning Star House, Inc. 505-232-8299

New Mexico Victims' Rights Project 888-410-1084

New York State Adult Domestic Violence Hotline English 800-942-6906 Spanish 800-942-6908 New York State Crime Victims Board Hotline 800-247-8035

New York City 24-Hour Hotlines Bilingual Hotline 800-621-HOPE; Hearing Impaired 800-810-7444

North Carolina Coalition Against Domestic Violence Phone: 919-956-9124 or 888 232-9124 FAX: 1-919-682-1449

North Carolina Crime Victim Compensation Services 800-826-6200

North Carolina Council for Women/Domestic Violence Commission 1320 Mail Service Center, Raleigh, North Carolina 27699-1320; 919-733-2455.

North Dakota Council On Abused Women's Services/Coalition Against Sexual Assault in ND. 418 East Rosser Ave #320, Bismarck, ND 58501-4046 Toll-free 888-255-6240 or 701-255-6240

North Dakota Domestic Violence Hotline North Dakota currently uses the National Domestic

Violence Hotline 800-799-SAFE (7233)

Ohio Domestic Violence Network, 4807 Evans Wood Drive, Suite 201, Columbus, Ohio 43229, 614-781-9651 614-781-9652 Fax 614-781-9654 TTY; Email: info@odvn.org

Ohio Coalition on Sexual Assault 4041 North High Street, Suite 408 Columbus, Ohio 43214, 614-268-3322

Oklahoma Statewide Safeline 800-522-7233

Oklahoma Coalition on Domestic Violence 405-524-0700

Oklahoma – Spirits of Hope (Native American) 405-619-9707

Oklahoma – Crime Victim Compensation 800-745-6098

Oregon Coalition Against Domestic & Sexual Violence 888-235-5333

Oregon Crime Victim Outreach Coordinator 503-378-5348

Oregon US Attorney Victim Assistance 503-727-1036

Oregon Victim-Witness Coordinator 503-224-4181

Oregon Sexual Assault Support Services, 591 West 19th Ave., Eugene, OR Crisis Line 800-788-4727 or 541-343-SASS

Pennsylvania Coalition Against Domestic Violence 800-932-4632

Pennsylvania Commission for Women 886-615-7477

Pennsylvania – Women In Transition 24-hour Hotline 215-751-1111

Pennsylvania Women Work 866-PAWOMEN or 412-281-9270

Rhode Island Coalition Against Domestic Violence 800-494-8100

Rhode Island – Sexual Assault & Trauma Center 401-421-4100 (call collect)

South Carolina Coalition Against Domestic Violence & Sexual Assault PO Box 7776, Columbia, SC 29202 Phone # 800-260-9293 Fax 803-256-1030

South Carolina Victim Assistance Network (SCVAN) 1900 Broad River Road, Suite 200, Columbia, SC 29210 803-750-1200 www.scvan.org

South Dakota Network Against Family Violence Phone 800-670-3989

South Dakota Coalition Against Domestic Violence 800-572-9196

South Dakota – Citizens Against Rape And Domestic Violence 300 North Dakota Ave. Suite 220, Sioux Falls, SD 57102 Phone 605-339-0116

Tennessee Coalition Against Domestic and Sexual Violence; PO Box 120972, Nashville, TN 37212, 800-289-9018.

Tennessee – www.tennhelp.com

Tennessee Domestic Violence Shelter Hotline – Hotline only, statewide 800-356-6767

Texas Council on Family Violence 512-794-1133

Texas – Crisis Center of Anderson & Cherokee Counties, PO Box 8371, Jacksonville, TX 75766; Hotline 800-232-8519 Phone 903-586-9118

Texas – Domestic Violence Prevention, 424 Spruce St., PO Box 712, Texarkana, TX 75501

Texas Health and Human Services Family Violence Program Hotline 800-799-7233

Texas - Women's Protective Services, PO Box 54089, Lubbock, TX 79453 Hotline 800-736-6491 or 806-747-6491.

Texas – Noah Project, PO Box 875, Abilene TX Hotline 800-444-3551 Hotline 325-676-7107

Utah – Statewide Toll-Free InfoLink 800-897-LINK 24 hrs a day

Utah Domestic Violence Council, 205 North 400 West, Salt Lake City, UT 84103 Tel 801-521-5544 Fax 801-521-5548 www.udvac.org

Utah Domestic Violence Advisory Council 700-897-5465

Vermont Network Against Domestic Violence 800-228-7395

Vermont – Advocacy for Immigrant Women 802-479-7547

Vermont - Sexual Violence Hotline 800-489-7273

Vermont Center for Crime Victim Services 800-750-1213

Virginia – Family Violence & Sexual Assault Hotline 24 hours a day 800-838-8238

Virginia Sexual and Domestic Violence Action Alliance 866-387-3822 www.vsdvalliance.org

Virginia Poverty Law Center Advocates on behalf of low-income Virginians on poverty issues. 800-868-8752 (Ext. 16 or ask for someone in the domestic violence unit) 804-782-9430 (ext 16 or

ask for someone in the domestic violence unit)
Virginia – Crime Victim Assistance 888-887-3418
Virginia – S.A.R.A The Sexual Assault Resource Agency, PO Box 6880, Charlottesville, VA 22906 Hotline 434-977-7273 Office 434-295-7273 Fax 434-220-4791
Virginia – Violence Intervention Program 703-246-3033
Washington State Coalition Against Domestic Violence – Seattle Office 1402 – 3rd Ave, Suite 406, Seattle, WA 98101 206-389-2515; 206-389-2520 Fax; 206-389-2900 TTY; Olympia Office 711 Capitol Way, Suite 702 Olympia, WA 98501 360-586-1022 phone; 360-586-1024 Fax; 360-586-1029 TTY
Washington Statewide 24-Hour Domestic Violence Hotline 800-562-6025
Washington's Violence Against Women Network WAVAWNet.org
Washington Law Help
WashingtonLawHelp.org
Washington – ProtectionOrder.org
www.protectionorder.org
West Virginia Statewide Coalition Against Domestic Violence 304-765-2250
West Virginia Legal Aid, 922 Quarrier Street, 4th floor, Charleston, WV 25301 304-343-4481 or 800-642-8279
Wisconsin Coalition Against Domestic Violence 800-799-7233

Wisconsin – Refugee Family Strengthening 608-267-7838

Wisconsin – UNIDOS Against Domestic Violence 800-451-6095

Wisconsin – American Indians Against Abuse 715-634-9980

Wyoming Coalition Against Domestic Violence & Sexual Assault, 409 S. 4th PO Box 236, Laramie, WY 82073 307-755-5481 Crisis Line 800-990-3877

Wyoming Crime Victims Center 888-707-8979

Wyoming – Civil Legal Assistance for Victims 800-990-3877

Author Contact

http://www.nocontactbook.com

References

http://samvak.tripod.com by Sam Vaknin, Ph.D.
http://www.halcyon.com/jmashmun/npd/dsm-iv.html
 1998-2004 by Joanna M. Ashmun